DREAM

**PRACTICAL ADVICE
FOR THE EVERYDAY DREAMER**

J. TAYLOR

Copyright © 2021 by Jeremy Taylor

All rights reserved. No part of this publication may be reproduced, distributed, or transmitted in any form or by any means, including photocopying, recording, or other electronic or mechanical methods, without the prior written permission of the publisher, except in the case of brief quotations embodied in critical reviews and certain other noncommercial uses permitted by copyright law.

The events and conversations in this book have been set down to the best of the author's ability. Every effort has been made to verify and correctly portray the information in this publication. The publisher will be pleased to make good any omissions or rectify any mistakes brought to their attention at the earliest opportunity.

Lead editor: Travers Johnson
Secondary editor: Krystle Taylor
Cover design by Brian Easley
Interior Design by KUHN Design Group

ISBN 978-1-7377482-0-5 (Paperback)
ISBN 978-1-7377482-1-2 (eBook)

First Edition

Published by Peak Publishing

shotsontaylor.com

*"Give a man a fish
and you feed him for a day.*

*Teach him how to fish
and you feed him for a lifetime."*

LAO TZU

CONTENTS

Preface: My Conversation with a Dying Man 9

Introduction 17

1. Finding Purpose 21
   Jason Gibson

2. Don't Quit Your Day Job 33
   Bria Celest

3. Pushing Past Anxiety 47
   Brian Easley

4. Embracing Failure 59
   Jordan Franklin, Esq.

5. Live Simply 73
   Kayland Partee

6. Make Your Own Lane 83
   Matthew Mayberry

7. Always Networking 97
   Ashlee Young

8. Financial Literacy 115
   Greg Brumfield, Esq.

Conclusion 131

Acknowledgments 137

*For my father, Alphonso "Rat" Taylor
Pops, because of you, I am free to dream.*

Preface

My Conversation with a Dying Man

It was a beautiful November day in 2017. The sun was out and there was a nice breeze. I was wearing some dusty blue slacks, a pair of beat up brown shoes, and a polo button-down I had owned since my freshman year in college. I'm positive my wife was embarrassed by my fashion sense [or lack thereof], but she stuck it out with me until things got better. I was dressed for success because I had an important lunch meeting with a potential mentor. Looking back on it, my family from the Delta would say I looked "thrown away." But, I felt good. Although my clothes were in terrible shape, this was the happiest I had been in years. I had recently quit a good job prematurely to chase money, freedom, and a dream. During that reckless stint I fell flat on my face, and life showed me a thing or two about debt, "following your passion," and the consequences of losing your reason. But now things were back on track, and I was beginning to see the light at the end of the tunnel of my bad decisions.

I was at the table conversing with my potential mentor when I received a fourth back-to-back phone call from my mother. After ignoring the previous three, I decided to answer. "Ma, I'm at a lunch meeting and I really can't talk," I said agitatedly.

In my arrogance, I thought everything was fine. I was too selfish to stop and think about why she would have called four times in a row, only thinking about this meeting and how I could benefit from its success. I couldn't have cared less what she had to say—or at least I thought.

"Jeremy!" she wailed when I finally answered. "We rushed your dad to the VA hospital; something with his heart isn't right." I froze. I couldn't think, I couldn't speak. She continued, "Are you there? What are you going to do?!"

The next few hours were a blur, but somewhere between packing, crying, and panicking, I ended up on Interstate 20 East headed to Jackson, MS from Dallas, TX. It was a drive that I was about to become all too familiar with; one that would be a part of some of the most defining moments of my life.

Let's backtrack: only five minutes prior, everything was just fine—or at least I was telling myself that it was. But now, as my world was being turned upside down, I began to question my happiness. It seemed like no matter how hard I tried, I would find my way to bad luck again. So here I was—at possibly the best job of my career, newly engaged, living a good life in a big city—and just like always, with one call I was spiraling again.

Maybe it was fate, but during the drive a question flashed across my mind, almost as if someone was speaking to me: "Are you truly happy?" For the rest of that drive I couldn't think of anything other than some variation of this question. Being trapped in a car had forced me to deal with my thoughts, so I began to self-assess. I realized instantly that I had been lying to myself; the answer was no. Buried in that "no" was a lot of debt, bad decisions, self-uncertainty, and dishonesty. Like most people, I thought that I could just wish my problems away. That never works, and if you gain nothing else from this book, gain this: problems don't go away; you either address them or they get worse and cause you more harm in the future.

As my dad remained hospitalized over the next five months, the drive to Jackson became like a meditation for me. I searched everywhere for the calmness I found on that road. That routine ride from Dallas to Jackson and back served as some of the most formative months of my life. During that time, I was particularly open to advice on how to improve my circumstances, and I stumbled across two things that would help me rebuild myself.

For the next five months, I listened to Nipsey Hussle's Grammy-nominated album *Victory Lap* and the classic book *Think and Grow Rich* by Napoleon Hill[1] on repeat. Between both of these works, I realized that validation must come from within and true change must also start there.

After my dad's second open heart surgery, he decided to throw in the towel. My mom and I were both devastated and angry, but I had decided that I was going to make one last plea with him to have the surgery. Before my plea I wanted to talk to the doctor to fully understand the implications of this surgery. Summed up, his aorta had another tear and this time it was not in a favorable direction. The physician said he would need another open heart surgery, and due to the recency of the

---

1. A quick note on Napoleon, as there is some controversy around his authenticity. For me, and I can only speak for myself, regardless of whether he was a crook or a scholar, the lessons in that book prove to be very valuable.

last surgery, the stakes were higher. I have immense respect for doctors because they have to say some hard things in a very direct way.

"Jeremy, there is a very high chance that your father dies on that table if we go through with this," she said. "There is also a chance that he lives, and I will make it my business for him to walk out of here. But let me be very direct with you: this will be a very risky surgery."

With all the facts intact, I went to my dad's room and pulled a chair up to his bedside. "What's up old man?" I began.

He grinned and replied, "Shit, I'm feeling old doc." I chuckled and looked into his eyes. I could see that he was drained. "You came down here again?!" he asked. "I told you that you needed to stay off that road."

"I'm good, Pops," I assured him. "I had to come check on you. Mom told me you don't want to have that surgery."

He cut me off in the coolest tone and said, "You know your mom is always spun up about something, doc. She calls herself mad at me because I don't want to do it. She says I'm being a coward and I'm quitting on her."

People—myself included—tend to overlook another person's discomfort for our own deeply selfish reasons. My father was in pain. Who were we to try to convince him that he should continue pushing, as if we had been the ones who had been opened up twice?

"Doc," he continued, "I raised you to be a man and to make your own decisions and never let another man or woman make them for you, right?"

"Yea…" I replied.

"Well that's what I'm asking you to let me do," he said. "I'm asking you to let one man make his own decision. I'm not scared. If anything, I'm brave. I'm tired of fighting, and it's time for me to face what's in front of me."

The tears begin to stream from my eyes, and I remember one dropping on his hand. He looked at me and said, "Stop crying, I'm going to be alright. I hate that I'm leaving you all like this, but I will be fine."

"Do something for me, doc. When I go, you cry, grieve, whatever you have to do to get all that pain out. But after a couple of days, you need to get up, dust yourself off, and keep on pushing.

Let me tell you something, life doesn't stop for nobody. You're gonna spend all your time crying over me—praying for it to all be a dream—only to wake up five years later to realize you have been sleepwalking through life, and I'm still gone."

The room was quiet. I held his hand and cried some more. He looked at me and said, "Doc, don't be like me; go chase your dream. When I came up, things were different. America was different, and I didn't understand things the way I do now. You got it in you. Don't let anyone tell you what you can't do. Whatever your dream—no matter how big—work for it and it's yours. At the end of the day, you have to give it everything you got so you can at least look yourself in the mirror and say you tried."

I broke down. In an attempt to clear my mind and escape the unfortunate reality of the situation, I hopped in my car and hit the road back to Dallas. As my mind began to drift, I realized that everything negative in my life was a product of a prior action that I had made. Excessive drinking and feeling sorry for myself kept me in a continuous state of low-grade depression, which kept me from making good decisions and doing what I knew needed to be done.

Overwhelmed with emotion, I pulled over in a vacant parking lot in Louisiana and sobbed. But I made a promise to myself that day: moving forward, I would never lose my sense of self or depend on anyone or anything else for validation. I would search for and live out my purpose. As I sat on the trunk of my car in some backwoods town, drinking a Coors Lite and watching the cars pass for about two hours, all my troubles seemingly began to fade away.

There has been no other moment in my life that inspires me more than the final conversation with my father. On that ride back to Dallas, it played in my head over and over. As I drove, I analyzed my past decisions—financially, relationally, and entrepreneurially. I told myself that if I was going to reach my full potential, I had to be honest with myself.

Without realizing it, this was the first time in the previous 10 years that I had actually stopped to assess the damage of the past decade. And it had been damaged. The road was littered with failed dreams, bad decisions, and a lot of self-inflicted pain. But in that moment, I made another vow to myself: I would begin my search for true happiness and I would seek a profession that aligned with my skills and what I really wanted to do. Although I'm not quite sure if I have completed my search for happiness, these last four years have brought me a lot of joy and reminded me of some valuable lessons I learned along the way.

In the coming pages you will read interviews that share stories, thoughts, or insights that I felt needed to be more widely spread. These stories provide valuable lessons that will help free your mind of some unnecessary baggage, while helping to shape your new journey.

Dream is special to me because it represents all of the action I have taken up to this point. It represents me following my dream. I'm older and wiser, but internally I'm still that little boy that has big dreams. Now, more than ever, I needed something to guide and push me.

Toni Morrison once said, "If there is a book that you want to read, but it hasn't been written yet, you must be the one to write it." This book is just that for me. It will serve as my personal "true north." No matter where my life takes me, I believe that if I remain in touch with the stories recounted in this book, I will always find peace of mind, guidance, and something to reignite my flame.

Most importantly, I believe my purpose in life is to communicate, and I want to start living in that purpose by communicating this information to anyone looking for sound advice. Good life advice shouldn't be hard, and this book will help simplify things.

I believe there is something in this book that can propel anyone forward; you just need a little patience, flexibility, and creativity. I hope that this book becomes for someone else what it has been for me: a guide to help you follow your dream.

INTRODUCTION

> *"It's hard to predict in advance
> what you'll grow to love."*
> **CAL NEWPORT**

Throughout this book, you will notice different questions that accompany each chapter. I want you to pay close attention to one in particular: "Passion or Skill?" This is important because *Dream* derived from this question. When I was looking for happiness and clarity, a good friend recommended a book that changed my life: *So Good They Can't Ignore You: Why Skills Trump Passion in the Quest for Work You Love* by Cal Newport. The main idea of the book can be summed up when Cal says, "'Follow your passion' is bad advice."

That statement struck me because prior to reading that book, I completely believed that finding your passion was the key to happiness. *So Good* sent me down the path of answering the question, "How do people end up loving what they do?" I was especially interested in this topic because I was coming off a personally exhausting search for my own passion. That search led me through chronic job-hopping, loads of depression, tons of wasted time, a ton of debt, and other problems I'm still working out with my therapist.

However, after my quiet and subtle search, I realized that the answer is actually quite simple: you don't have to choose passion or skill, but it is critical to understand that passion alone won't bring you happiness. It has to be coupled with some sort of skill. The dream life you are seeking can only be sustained with something that can't be taken away from you, and that something is your skillset. Sure, there are exceptions to the rule, but for the everyday dreamer like you and me, it's best we depend on ourselves. Passion doesn't strike you like a jolt of energy one day, nor does skill come from aimlessly putting 10,000 hours into something meaningless to you and your peace of mind. I found that true passion comes from you taking a skill that you are naturally good at, or something you enjoy doing, and making a constant and continual effort to build on it. Take some time to evaluate yourself by looking internally for traces of what you are good at, and even revisiting and reconnecting with your youth to help bring clarity to your search.

When I began self-evaluating, I decided it was time for me to stop running from the one thing I was always gifted at: communicating. I have always had a knack for relating to and understanding people on a deeper level, and I decided to use my skills to interview others and provide value to the public. Once I stopped resisting and focused my energy towards refining my skill, things began to get calmer and my sense of purpose started to become clearer. Without even realizing it, I had become insanely passionate about my work: spending hours on the road to conduct interviews; sending countless emails to potential interviewees; and moving my schedule around to accommodate those who will take the time to talk with me.

I started this journey with one goal in mind: to interview people I respected and ask them that simple question, "What's more important to achieve the personal and professional life of your dreams: passion or skill?" However, what started out as a simple question blossomed into a broader search to "pick the brain" of other dreamers, which resulted in me interviewing numerous people and ultimately deciding to write this book.

> "People who tell you to follow your passion are already rich." **—Scott Galloway**

So let's get down to practical matters.

WHAT IS *DREAM*?

Dream is a book that compiles practical tips from a diverse group of creators, professionals, executives, and everyday dreamers who have pushed through various situations or exhibit some quality that can be universally applied. This book is designed to inspire growth and provide meaningful and actionable ideas.

WHO IS THIS BOOK FOR?

Otto Von Bismark once said, "Only a fool learns from his own mistakes. The wise man learns from the mistakes of others."

I wanted insight into how practical minds went about achieving success or dealing with the daily grind of seeking success. I then wanted to take that information and pass it along to you so that we can all make strides towards our goals.

So this book is for everyone. Whether you're chasing your dream or just looking for advice to improve your circumstances, this book can help. All it takes is some patience and creativity to mold an idea, or a helpful tip to fit your particular situation. You will find advice on the next move to make, the questions you should be asking, how to find your purpose, steps to overcome failure, and more.

WHY SHOULD YOU TAKE MY ADVICE?

In short, don't. Profit from the experience, wisdom, and mistakes of others. I have carefully selected each profile with the goal to provide well-rounded advice that will cover the whole gamut. The collective experience in the pages that follow can be applied to many of life's most common challenges. All you have to do is free yourself of any expectations and open your mind to the stories and advice from these eight guests.

> "The heart of human excellence often begins to beat when you discover a pursuit that absorbs you, frees you, challenges you, or gives you a sense of meaning, joy, or passion." **–Terry Orlick**

CHAPTER 1

FINDING PURPOSE

Jason "JG" Gibson

Instagram: @iamjasongibson

"If you find purpose, focus will find you."

How does one find purpose? This question led me on a search for a unique perspective, and I found it by sitting down with my old friend, Jason "JG" Gibson.

Initially, I thought our convo would be centered around religion. "I'm speaking as a Christian man, so my basis is the Bible," Jason said early in the interview. In that moment, it felt like I was about to receive a sermon rather than actionable answers, but I was completely wrong. JG isn't a guy that's going to "BibleThump" you to death; in nearly every discussion we had about religion, he offered only practical suggestions. The conversation blossomed like a flower, and it became clear why he has achieved so much over the last decade.

Jason is the poster child for high energy. When I was trying to schedule this interview he said, "Saturday would be best for me because it's the only day I'm not up at 5 AM." Somewhere in his daily allotment of 24 hours, Jason finds the time to be an entrepreneur, motivational speaker, and recording artist. But even more impressive is the fact that he is excelling at them all.

However, he wasn't always so focused. Like most teens, Jason spent the first years after high school finding himself, which led to a short-lived career as a small-time weed dealer. After suffering from a bad car accident and being robbed at gunpoint, he decided things had to change. "God was showing me that my sin will lead to my demise," he said. "It was a wake-up call for me to follow God."

After his commitment to change, Jason describes the following years as "unpredictable" because he had no idea he would be involved in his current ventures. His initial goal was to be a K-12 teacher and then become a university president, but after a short stint in education, he realized it was not for him. "Nothing in me wants to work in public education in that capacity anymore," he said. This trial by fire helped to improve his self-awareness, which ultimately fed his hunger to find and pursue his purpose.

Jason is transparent and forthcoming throughout this interview. "There's not much I hide," he said. "If I can give some advice, I will, because I genuinely want everybody to win."

He continued, "I give of myself and I like to teach and I work hard to create spaces where I can do that." When I approached Jason, I was torn on the theme of this piece. I continued to go back and forth in the days leading up to this interview thinking, "Focus or Purpose?"

As I told him on the day we spoke, "I think you have a level of focus that people can learn from." I continued, "I just see a guy that's active in church and co-manages a gym, all while running a successful clothing line. So how do you do it?"

Before I let him answer I decided to ask my question a bit more directly. "Do you think your success has been a byproduct of focus?" He quickly interjected and stated that his focus is actually a byproduct of knowing his purpose. "If you find purpose, focus will find you," he explained.

In his view, you can't help but to be focused on the things you are purposed to do and passionate about. In his life, things shifted into overdrive when he started doing more of what he loved. At that point, focus found him.

So what's Jason's specific purpose? He describes it this way. "I believe I was placed here to strengthen every fiber of a person's being. I do this through three specific niches: mental, physical, and spiritual."

Jason has carved out a lane in each niche. He helps people find mental strength through his speaking engagements, "Motivational Mondays" via Instagram and by tapping into his educational background. He helps people achieve physical strength through his boot camp-style fitness company Xplicit J3. Lastly, and perhaps most passionately, he strives to spiritually strengthen people through his ministry as the Director of Worship Arts at his church.

> "I think purpose is an ever evolving thing. Purpose is in the middle of the spectrum, nestled between calling and destiny."

Jason believes that purpose is found in helping people. But for him, purpose is just one step in a three-part life process. "I think purpose is an ever-evolving thing," he explained. "Purpose is in the middle of the spectrum, nestled between calling and destiny."

> **Calling:** We each receive assignments throughout life; we can be assigned to certain seasons, people, etc.. These assignments clarify your calling, which illuminates your purpose.
>
> **Purpose:** Passion that has been defined and cultivated. This leads to destiny.
>
> **Destiny:** This is your life's end goal. The ultimate thing for which people will remember you.

To begin this process of discovery, simply ask yourself, "What do I like to do?" Once you have your answer, the next step is plain: build on what you enjoy doing. True passion comes from building skills around something you naturally enjoy, not something that's forced. As Jason puts it, "As you build on what you enjoy, passion will follow. What follows passion is a sharpened skill." Following this formula can open doors in this digital era. The world is becoming more expansive and more inclusive, which presents us with endless opportunities.

I hope you enjoy this interview with my dear old friend Jason Gibson.

What advice do you have for people reading this chapter looking for purpose?

Ask yourself, "What do I like to do?" It's truly that simple: figure out what you like to do, then figure out how you can build on that. When you build on your passion, you will inevitably develop a sharpened skillset.

You can take almost anything and transform it into something tangible. For example, my little cousin is in high school and she told me that she wants to be a YouTuber. I told her to go for it, because in the current environment she can make as much, if not more, than a teacher or some government official. I told her that whatever she decides to do, just do it and do it well.

I'm not trying to sound poetic, but a lot of us forfeit our dreams and throw away our purpose because we are scared of the naysayers. Especially those who say, "Everybody is already doing that; why do you want to do it?" But to me, there's nothing wrong with being a copycat, as long as you copy the right cat. I think as long as you are extracting things from the right people, just do it. You are inevitably going to do something someone else is doing. The key is not to focus on the direction, but on staying in your lane. Focus on being more efficient and producing a better product than your competitor. My thought is always, "How can I do this better than the next man?"

> "The meaning of life is to find your gift. The purpose of life is to give it away." **–Picasso**

As a Christian, is there anything you hear about spirituality that you don't agree with?

Personally, I don't like the picture of this unattainable goal of perfection that Christianity presents. I'm talking specifically about the concept of salvation, which is what the Christian faith revolves around. Basically, it's about being saved from your sins and saved from yourself; about coming to, acknowledging, and submitting to Jesus Christ as your Lord and Savior. I think the narrative that we convey is that you have to be ready to give your life to Christ, become a Christian, or get stronger in your faith first. So, a lot of people carry this subconscious or unconscious narrative that they have to get themselves to a certain place before they can start going to church. It's like, "Man I gotta stop smoking weed before I can go back to church;" or "Bruh, I just need to smash three more chicks, then I'm gonna start going back to church;" or "I just can't stop lusting—I'll come to church once I get myself together."

That logic is faulty. The foundation of our faith leans on the belief that you can't get yourself together by yourself. There is no such thing as "being ready" to become a Christian, nor is there a perfect time to start going to church. That's the worst advice I hear, and it's the worst narrative that we force feed to people who aren't of the faith. We try to coach them into perfection before they come, but if you can make yourself perfect and fix yourself on your own, then you don't need the church or Christ.

Take me, for example. I am a heterosexual man. I love women. I lust over women's bodies and struggle with sex, lustful thoughts, and adoring women to the point of idolizing them. I have come to the realization that this is something I can't overcome by myself. That's why I, personally, need a savior.

I need a guide; I need instruction for how I can navigate these feelings that I don't know how to control. The Bible and the church serve as my instruction for continuing to get and keep myself together.

Do you believe in fate or that a person shapes their own destiny?

I do believe that, to an extent, we control our own destiny. I think we dictate how much or how little we extract from this life. It's obvious that I'm a Christian, but I think there are three wills for our lives: God's, the Enemy's, and our own. It's an ongoing search for which one we will gravitate towards. I think each will has a specific way of presenting itself, and how we interact with each makes all the difference. Ultimately, people grow in whatever they believe in. My opinion is that you and your faith determine what your end goal will be.

In terms of mental health, what's a stigma that gets under your skin?

That you don't need any mental reconciliation from an external resource like therapy or counseling to reach a healthy mental space. I go to therapy, but that's something that is often stigmatized. As a whole, we all deal with some level of mental trauma or dysfunction. Some people are able to work it out on their own, but many can't, and the trauma and dysfunction end up eating away at them. People should address their past, present, and potential future traumas. You have to talk about these things, because the quicker you become aware of them, the quicker you can address and put them behind you. I recommend therapy and self-reflection.

Can you give an example of how therapy has helped you overcome some of your internal challenges?

It's funny we got on the topic of mental reconciliation. I have a story that depicts exactly what I mean about how learning and dealing with your past can help you understand things about yourself. I usually train at my gym in the morning from 5-7 am, and I workout with my more advanced class from 7-8 am. Sometimes we do what's called a "MetCon," which is basically a series of exercises you do for time. It's intended to be competitive, and anybody that knows me knows I really hate losing. It doesn't matter what it is, I will harp on it and I won't let it go until you face me again. So this particular day, I tweaked my hamstring and I lost. Inside, I was furious. I decided to take the team to breakfast, hoping it would help me deal with it. But instead, I just kept talking about it the entire time we ate. I just kept saying things like, "Bro, you know you wouldn't have beat me if I was 100%."

Finally, one of the girls that was with us said, "Jason, let it go! Why are you such a sore loser?"

Before I could even catch myself the truth slid out. "The lack of validation from my father growing up," I replied. "I always feel like I have something to prove."

When I uttered those words it caught everyone by surprise, but it was the truth. This was something I wasn't conscious of until I hashed it out with my therapist. It just speaks to the previous point. We have so many shortcomings that we aren't aware of; but the quicker we can find the root of them, the quicker we can be delivered from them.

What's one negative quality people might say that you have?

I'm hard on my friends. Most people who see my social media persona would think, "I want to be connected to him." But the truth is, that's social media—I control that narrative so obviously I'm going to post my best image. A lot of times people see me and think "He's a motivational speaker, preacher, business owner, and real estate investor—I need a guy like that in my circle." Don't be fooled. My friends will tell you, I'm very forward with them. I'm not looking for "yes" men; I want the raw criticism and the truth and that's exactly what I give. I don't believe in selling dreams. I want to redirect my friends and people in general to what they are purposed to do. I remember one time I was about to release a song and one of my true friends told me, "That song isn't good, you can do better."

So how do you do better? What processes do you incorporate to produce your best work?

For me, it's all about "Pray, Plan, Execute." I pray, and out of prayer I develop a plan, and out of my plan, I execute. In the church, we often go to prayer and stop there. We pray and say, "Ok, Lord, do your thing," and nothing happens after that. And then, you have some people who will pray and plan, but never execute. I have friends who have been writing a book for 10 years, or have songs recorded that have never been heard. People spend years in school to get all these degrees, but never even step into their field.

I named my fashion line *Play, Plan, Execute* because I'm trying to get people to buy into that lifestyle. When I first started people were saying, "Why do you want to start a clothing line?

Everybody's starting a t-shirt line." If I listened to those people, I literally wouldn't be doing anything I'm doing right now. I saw and supported all the clothing lines in Jackson, but I asked myself, "How can I make mine different?" For me, it wasn't about selling clothes, but selling a lifestyle. Other designs may look better than mine and other people may market better than me, but at the end of the day, I'm not trying to sell fashion, I want you to live your life by pray, plan and execute.

What's the best advice a parent ever gave you?

It definitely came from my mom, she was extremely supportive. To this day, she supports everything I do, but the best advice she ever gave me was a scripture: "His lord said unto him, Well done, good and faithful servant; thou hast been faithful over a few things, I will make thee ruler over many things…" (Matthew 25: 23)

Summed up, this means be faithful in the small things and you will be ruler over the big things. Faithfully get up on time; faithfully study and go to school; faithfully perfect your craft, etc. Do that and you will have an abundance of things at your disposal.

Do you have any book recommendations?

Am I Called? by Dave Harvey and Matt Chandler
From Weakness to Strength by Scott Sauls
Black Privilege by Charlamagne tha God

What is more important: passion or skill?

I'd say they are equally important. Passion comes from purpose and skill comes from being passionate about your purpose.

What's one skill people can adopt from you?

Being multifaceted. I've always been good at becoming what I need to be in the moment. With my gym, because I had the most polished business acumen, I transitioned and became the CEO. I handle all the business, finances, and the allocation of funds because that's where I'm the strongest right now within our three-fold dynamic of people. At my church, I'm the worship leader, but if I need to become the preacher, I'll preach. If I need to become the administrator, I'll become that. If you need me to be the parking attendant, I'll become that too. I've been blessed with the trait of becoming whatever I need to become in the moment.

Just curious; what's one piece of advice for people who don't want to work out?

Just walk. Staying active will solve a lot of problems. If you don't workout and you feel like you can't do anything, just walk and stay active.

Any last words?

God doesn't call the equipped, he equips the called.

> "You can't always control your feelings, but you can control your focus" **–Steven Furtick**

CHAPTER 2

DON'T QUIT YOUR DAY JOB

Bria Celest aka "The Queen of Vacay"
Instagram: @queenofvacay | Twitter: @55mmbae
"There are riches in the niches."

In my opinion, "foodies" typically have terrible taste. When it comes to food, I am a "prove it" kind of guy. But I must give credit where it's due—Bria Celest has a food palate that is spot on. We met before COVID-19 swept the country and I must say, she showed me some pretty nice spots. Our interview took place in Dallas, TX, where the restaurants we ate and conversed at included Magnolias Sous Le Pont, a quaint coffee shop where we enjoyed a croissant, and Whistle Britches, where we had their fried chicken and a couple of drinks. As if that wasn't enough, we concluded with a Popsicle from a cute shop called Picolé.

Here's the thing: she takes her food experiences very seriously. She commented several times, "I won't eat at a restaurant if they don't have at least 4 stars on Yelp." Not only is she a serious foodie, but the self-proclaimed "Queen of Vacay" is a photographer and travel blogger.

So who exactly is Bria? Hailing from Alaska, she's the second oldest of eight siblings and considers herself a bubbly, outgoing know-it-all, whose go-with-the-flow spirit is clearly shown through her dislike of long-term planning. But if you want to talk about something that sparks her interest, look no further than Twitter. She's been on the platform since 2009 and has built a loyal following that she prefers to refer to as a community. For her, it's not about the followers, but it's always been a way of expressing her thoughts.

During this interview, we discussed a broad range of topics including photography and her travel blog, but most notably, quitting her job. The latter was important to me because countless people struggle with determining when is the right time to walk away. After following her for a few weeks on Twitter, I decided she would be the ideal person to speak with about not quitting your day job prematurely to pursue your passion. In theory, it's cool to up and quit, but if the proper steps haven't been taken, you will find yourself in a load of pain and emotional turmoil.

So let's get started. As a self-taught photographer, I often look at the work of my peers to improve my own. Bria is a talented photographer and she has taken gorgeous photos that I dream to take. Her angles are intriguing and her ability to pose her clients in flattering ways is top-tier. Therefore, to break the ice and ease into the conversation, my first question was simple: how did you develop your photography skills? Her answer: "I honed in on a style and worked consistently at perfecting it."

During that period, which was her first year of photography, money and fame weren't the focus. Instead, she was committed to building her portfolio and developing her skills. She purchased her first camera (a Nikon D5000) and challenged herself to shoot daily. Since then, she has photographed for many high profile brands, countless models, and occasionally, weddings. You would think that makes her a camera junkie, but she is actually quite the opposite. She generally prefers to shoot with her iPhone due to her minimalist style and disdain for carrying equipment. "It's convenient and I don't like to have my hands tied up," she said.

These days she doesn't bother to obsess over the latest camera gear; in her mind there is only one question when it comes to photography, "Does it take pictures or not?"

Starting out, the goal was simple: learn to take nice pictures. But after noticing she could make money and travel, it quickly became more. Her flexible schedule—working one week on and one week off—provided her room to dream. Excited, she decided to travel to Chicago with the sole purpose of photographing the architecture. Although her job and travel schedule blended beautifully, she is adamant that your schedule shouldn't stop you from traveling. "You just have to do shorter trips and those work better for some people," she explained.

Writing a travel blog was not what she initially sought to do. She began by giving travel advice on Twitter, mainly through threads. As the questions from her community became repetitive, she saw an excellent opportunity to launch her own travel blog. This gave her the ability to centralize her travel content and the answers to frequently asked questions.

Bria is a prime example of the magic that can happen when opportunity meets preparation. Her travel journey began back in 2016 when she took her first trip to Tokyo. Since then she's traveled to Greece, Cuba, Vietnam, Italy, and many other countries. Before COVID-19 brought the travel industry to its knees in the early part of 2020, she was taking roughly 50 flights a year and traveling at least twice a month.

As soon as things return to normal, you will likely catch her heading to a big city that offers good food, culture, and plenty of photo ops. So I asked her, "Do you have a strategy when visiting these cities?"

"Nope," she replied. "Sometimes the Airbnbs I rent are small and you end up relaxing, and sometimes you don't have enough time for everything." What we do know is the strategy to deliver quality content to her community is running smoothly. Her "Trippin" guides provide information on finding cheap flights and accommodations, as well as budgeting tips and travel hacks. She is growing her brand as a travel blogger and photographer right in front of our eyes.

So, what's next for Bria? She is admittedly bad at forward thinking, but in the short-term she would like to continue to grow her blog. Maybe she'll go back to rolling cigars in Cuba or photographing Japan during cherry blossom season. Whatever it is, she is looking forward to traveling and enjoying good times with good food and good people.

Here are some of my favorite parts of my interview with Bria.

What steps did you take to build your brand before quitting your job?

- Step 1: Build Your Audience
- Step 2: Tailor Your Content

- Step 3: Be Consistent
- Step 4: Monetize

STEP 1: BUILD YOUR AUDIENCE

You have to start by building an audience. Obviously to do that there are a lot of branches. To keep it simple, I think the easiest place to start is knowing and understanding your audience. I use my analytics on Instagram and Twitter a lot. For instance, my audience consists of quite a few men. So when I shoot men, those shots might not perform as well as the ones I do with women. Everyone likes looking at a pretty woman, but not everyone wants to see an attractive guy. Basically, you just need to listen and pay attention to what your audience likes.

You also have to interact with them. Your goal should be to interact with your followers and audience through a form of storytelling that's true to you. In order to grow your brand, you have to start cultivating that interaction. I call it "The J. Cole Syndrome." I don't think he makes good music, but people relate to him, and relatability is key. People want to support a brand that's real and authentic. That's a big part of my personal brand: to my audience, I feel like a real person, because I am.

STEP 2: TAILOR YOUR CONTENT

You have to tailor your content. Once you have built your audience, you need to listen to them and review your analytics to understand what content is working. Another thing you can do is ask your followers what they want to see. I do this often before I get ready to publish one of my guides. I ask them what cities they would like to see or what questions they have. At the end of the day, there's no point in making content no one wants to see.

STEP 3: BE CONSISTENT

This is pretty straightforward. You don't have to post every day, but posting consistently keeps your brand relevant.

STEP 4: MONETIZE

The last thing is figuring out how to make money. If this is something you want to turn into a job after you've taken the other steps, it's time to figure out a way to monetize. There really isn't a step-by-step on this because every brand is different. Just follow the previous general guidelines and tweak them so they work for you.

How do you build relationships with customers while building your brand?

People like people that they can relate to; people who they feel are personable. People are more likely to support you if they like you as a person, so being rude or snappy to potential customers can be really bad for business. You can't allow potential customers to see that because you don't know who's going to see it or how it's going to be perceived. Perception is really important, especially online. Even if you didn't mean something in a rude way it can be perceived as such, so you have to be careful with your words. I'm always trying to tailor my responses so I don't come off as a jerk.

I'm very sarcastic, but sarcasm is very hard to convey through online interactions. People will read it and think you are being rude when that's not the case. I see it all the time: people say a business owner was rude and then they say I'm not going to support that person again. Since I was a kid, I've always lived by treating people how you want to be treated. However, I totally get it—I know it gets frustrating as a brand, business owner, or influencer. People always feel entitled to your time and you're constantly answering the same questions over and over again. I understand being irritated, but you have to contain yourself. If you aren't in a good mood, just don't reply.

> "I've learned that people will forget what you said, people will forget what you did, but people will never forget how you made them feel." **—Maya Angelou**

When you were new to photography, how did you grow your business?

The first year I was doing photography, I didn't charge anything or make any money. I just wanted to build a portfolio because nobody is going to work with someone who doesn't have any experience. In the beginning, you need experience; that's more important than knowing every little setting on the camera. I was constantly messaging people on Instagram and tweeting things like, "Hey, any models wanna shoot?" It was just for fun and practice at first, but before I knew it I was getting a lot of work off of those shoots.

Looking back on it, those shoots gave me a bulk of my

practice and from them I really started to see my skills improve. You're not going to improve if you aren't shooting. If this is your craft and your livelihood, you need to make money from it, but you are not going to get booked if you don't have any work to show. You can't build skills unless you practice. You can read and watch as many tutorials as you want, but if you're not out actively shooting, you're never going to get better. That goes for photography or any other skill.

Why was it important for you to put an emphasis on cost-efficient travel?

I felt like most people could relate to the idea of traveling on a budget versus luxury travel. Most people are your average 9-5 job workers, and those are the people I could relate to. I'm not rich, but I've been able to travel pretty frequently. Growing up, my family wasn't poor, but we weren't super well off by any means. Like I told you, I came from a house of 8 kids and we were raised and lived off of a military salary, so I've always had to have a cost-efficient mindset. I always felt like most people didn't have a ton of money to spend on things like travel, so for me, it felt better to talk about what I knew and could relate to. My biggest goal was and still is showing others how to travel affordably, but without sacrificing comfort.

When you were quitting your job, what fears and anxieties did you have?

I was definitely a little worried. I'm someone who likes to work and am used to having money at my disposal. So initially, I just kept thinking about how I would make money. I'm pretty "boujee" and I have expensive taste, so there was no way I was just going to be scrounging for dollars. I was nervous about money, but weirdly I was even more worried about what I would do with all this free time. Once you quit your job, you realize how much time you spend there, especially me because I was spending half a day at work. I also worried if I was going to be successful. The thought of failing made me nervous. I mean, I'm still worried about failing, but at some point it's now or never.

Were your parents supportive when you quit your job?

For the most part, my parents are very supportive. But when I was first contemplating the idea of quitting my job they were concerned. "Why would you do that?," they questioned. "Your life is good. You have guaranteed money and benefits, you know your schedule, and you are still doing what you want to do on the side. Why would you give all of that up to go into this abyss of maybe?"

It was a totally valid argument and both of my parents are in their 50s, so they come from a different time. People from that era didn't just quit a good job to go do some hobby, so to them, it was a foreign concept. But as I kept them informed on how well my books were doing and how I was making more money doing this than I was making at my job, they started to become ok with it. They started telling me to do whatever was going to make me happy and they started fully supporting me.

My mom is my biggest supporter. She buys all of my books. Although she could just ask me for them, she makes it a point to buy them, always saying things like, "Now my collection is complete."

What's more important: passion or skill?

Skill, for sure. I'm a very practical and logical thinker. I'm not saying people who think differently than me are illogical; I'm just saying I think skill is the most important of the two. To me, if you are bad at something but you really love it, so what. I love painting, but I'm bad at it, so I'm not going to start selling my paintings just because I love them.

The thing about skill is this: even if you don't like something you are skilled at, at least you can make money off of it. What I'm saying is, being bad at something and really loving it doesn't get you anywhere. At the end of the day your skills are going to get you paid, but your passion might not.

How did you grow your photography skills?

For me, it was mostly honing in on a style and doing that style consistently. Also making sure things were aesthetically sound. I plan out my shoots and I think more people should start planning theirs. Things like what's going to look good, what's going to fit the theme we are going for, how the model/client is going to be dressed, etc. I also ask my client what type of photos they are going for. For example, if a client tells me they are going for an elegant style, I probably want to stay away from public parks.

Something simple that I did to get better was practice daily. I made it a goal and challenged myself to shoot every day, even if it was for only 15 minutes. This is a good way to build content and keep people engaged.

What advice would you give about quitting your job to pursue a passion?

When I first started photography, I wasn't making any

money the first year. My regular job was fueling what became my passion. That's why I always say, if you can do both, why not do it? Most of the time, people feel like they need to quit their job, but that's because it's cool and trendy right now.

Take my advice: don't quit with no money saved up. When I quit my job, I had savings because in freelance, you have to be prepared for the bookings to dry up. The nature of it is sometimes people just don't want to buy what you are selling at the moment. Freelancing has its ups and downs; nothing is guaranteed and nobody owes you anything.

One of my pet peeves is people saying, "I just quit my job, please support me!" You should have already built that support, so when you do quit, people already support you. Again, it's trendy to do, but when the dry spells hit, they are humbling. Save the, "I quit my job with six nickels—HELP!" stories. I'm not interested; no one told you to quit. That's why I say you should start by just doing your side hustle in your free time.

Let's use photography as an example. Most people work Monday–Friday from 9–5, so that gives you time to service most of your bookings on the weekends. So why can't you maintain your day job and do sessions on the weekends or after work? Sure you will be working a lot, but if it's something you want to do, you'll devote the time to it. If you really like what you are doing, is it that bad or that much of a hassle to do it in your free time on the weekend? It should be easy.

Any last words of advice you would like to offer?

Find a niche and stick with it. There are truly riches in the niches.

AUTHOR NOTE:

"Should I quit my Job?" This is a question that torments so many new entrepreneurs and dreamers, which is why when I saw Bria tweeting about quitting her job, I knew I wanted to interview her. Before I found my way to writing and journalism, I tried several different ventures that left me heartbroken and beaten down. I fell so in love with my dream that it clouded my judgement which led me to the irrational decision of prematurely quitting a really good job. Although I look back on that decision as being one of the best that I made, it still doesn't change the fact that in the moment, it was the wrong decision. The poor timing of my decision took years to overcome.

The point of this chapter isn't to discourage you from quitting your job, but to encourage you to think about the decision rationally. Close out the outside noise, sit with your favorite album, and really think through the decision before you make it. My hope is that Bria's advice will help you think about the entire picture before you walk out. I know; you don't want to work for "the man" and you want to be your own boss. You envision yourself quitting, making more money, and having a better quality of life without the stress of having to get up daily to build someone else's dream.

There is nothing wrong with that vision, but I think of it this way: you can game the system to work for you if you just have a little patience. Take the money and resources that your employer is providing and put it into your business or dream. In a way, it's like having them finance it. While your job takes a portion of your day and time to work for them, you take the compensation that they are providing and make that work for you. Make no mistake, walking out is the goal many of us have, but make sure you have your affairs in order before you do so.

> "It is not the strongest of the species that survive, nor the most intelligent, but the one most responsive to change." **—Charles Darwin**

CHAPTER 3

PUSHING PAST ANXIETY

Brian "EZ" Easley

Instagram & Twitter: @ezwuzhere

"Every opportunity is the opportunity for a greater opportunity."

Anxiety affects over 40 million adults in the United States yearly, making it one of the most common obstacles Americans face. I initially profiled Brian Easley or "EZ," because I was interested in his apparel industry experience. The advice and tips came as a byproduct of my preparation, but the enlightenment on the subject of anxiety colored my notes. It's worth mentioning that EZ is my brother-in-law, which is why some would assume I interviewed him. However, that is not the case.

To start, he and a good friend have been in a successful partnership since 2013. Brian also runs Illogic Creative, a personal venture in which he doubles as a photographer and creator. But it was his newest venture, All Good Thingx, that caught my attention. Why? Because it's founded on Brian's desire to combat anxiety.

"Anxiety is your body's natural response to stress," says Healthline.com, "it's a feeling of fear or apprehension about what's to come." We all know people who struggle with anxiety, but I admit, I never took the time to understand it. That ignorance made this interview ideal. It was EZ's answer to a random follow-up question that sparked my interest.

"How do you push forward when faced with a jolt of anxiety?" I asked him.

"By staying positive and trying to live in the moment," he replied. "Being in the moment for 'us' is harder than people realize; it takes real effort."

For me, being in the moment is easy; but throughout this interview, I learned that the concept of being present shouldn't be taken for granted.

It was around 2013 when Brian began actively building his design skills. Later that year, he and his longtime friend, Thaddeus Reed (Instagram:@boujienupe), formed a partnership and decided to grow Reed Enterprise (Instagram: @reedent). His partner was operating a t-shirt printing business, but the designs needed life.

As Brian recalls it, "The timing was perfect. I felt comfortable growing and trying things, and it served as a great opportunity to experiment."

That same year, they gained steam when the two decided to tackle a problem. At the time, Jackson State University's apparel was outdated; it lacked swag and didn't appeal to the younger crowd. ReedEnt exploited that niche, and by doing so grew their business tenfold. Brian credits the growth to their consistency, noting, "Most often, it's not what you can build, it's how many times you can rebuild it." Though successful now, Brian admits that things weren't always this fluid. In the beginning, anxiety clouded his mind.

Brian dealt with strong feelings of anxiety when he started his creative journey. He used to think, "I'm not classically trained," and those thoughts made him shrink. This is something a lot of creatives battle, so how do you get past that feeling? His advice is simple: "By starting."

It was 2012 when he got the idea to buy a camera and begin creating. His friend Aaron Thompson provided him access to several Adobe programs; a value of roughly $1,500. Influenced by Aaron, who now is the Director of Athletics Content Development at the University of Texas at Austin, Brian began building his creative foundation. Aaron told EZ, "I saw how hungry you were, and sometimes you just need a little push to get going."

EZ is quite the perfectionist, and mixing that with anxiety caused him some serious pain. He felt he was the only person who had the compulsive thoughts, "I'm not ready; it's not ready." But those thoughts are a precise example of anxiety. In its simplest form, anxiety is putting a lot of energy into thinking that everything that could go wrong will. His recipe for overcoming said thoughts is simple: "Relax and let your experience guide you; trust yourself."

He still uses that advice across the board, most notably when he's trying to settle into shooting an event. For example, EZ found himself frustrated while shooting at a Drake concert because he couldn't quite grasp the concept he was going for. So he stopped, took a breather, relaxed, and let his experience take the wheel. Naturally, this led to a spread of exceptional photos.

In 2013, Brian launched his personal company Illogic

Creative. "Illcreate" is a flip on what EZ wants the company to embody: "I'll Create." He explained, "I'm going to use my tools and 'I'll create' something tailored to you." He has provided branding services to a full gamut of entrepreneurs—from DJs to boutique owners—all with a focus on quality. EZ believes it's important that potential customers understand what you do. You have to be clear about your scope and understand that everybody is not your customer. In Brian's words, "Never sacrifice quality. People that want good quality will pay for it." But I wondered, if quality is the simple answer, why do clothing lines seldom work?

"Clothing is a hard space; you have to get intimate with it to make it work," he explained. Intimacy is what makes EZ's current venture, All Good Thingx, a natural fit. What makes this line special is the specific focus. Curbing anxiety starts with taking a deep breath and indulging in good thoughts, more specifically, indulging in All Good Thingx. Personally, I was impressed with the design and the packaging, which is exactly what he wants his customers to feel.

"When people buy my stuff, I don't want them to feel 'sold.' I want them to be happy with the purchase," he said. "I respect people's money. They could spend anywhere, so I strive to provide them with consistency and peace of mind." Considering that he personally packs, folds, and tags every item that is sent out, he is doubling down on ensuring that customers feel good.

In a blog published on December 29, 2015, Brian wrote, "Every opportunity is the opportunity for a greater opportunity." As dreamers, we can find solace in those words. For brevity, I paraphrased Brian's closing thoughts. If you are going to be successful, you have to take the chance. You have to get comfortable with being uncomfortable, and the sooner you learn you're different, the better. Don't feel sorry for yourself. Be honest and understand who you are. That starts with being real with yourself and understanding your strengths and weaknesses. Understand how they can hold you back, or potentially, propel you forward.

I wrote this piece because someone needed to hear it, and I appreciate EZ for being vulnerable. Whoever you are, I hope this moves you to act.

Here are some of my favorite questions from my chat with my "bro," EZ.

What would you tell someone dealing with anxiety?

You have to get out of your own head and understand you're not alone. When I told people what I was dealing with, a lot of them didn't really believe it, or—in their defense—they didn't understand it. The key to getting out of your own head is realizing that sometimes the reality we create internally isn't real. A lot of times, we are the root of our problems; we can sometimes trick ourselves into thinking negatively. You can't avoid situations because they make you anxious. If it's gotta be done it's gotta be done. Face it with that lump in your throat, but it's good to understand what you are feeling and why you are feeling it. It's really a mind over matter thing.

You once tweeted, "Twitter makes everyone think they can be an entrepreneur." Could you explain what you mean?

Daymond John is someone I get a lot of information and motivation from. His book *The Power of Broke* is one of my favorites. He talks a lot about how people will shame you for keeping your day job. They say things like, "Ahh, you're not a real entrepreneur, you still have a job." He always uses the story of him working at Red Lobster for five years until he got FUBU off the ground. In that story he talks about how he wasn't making much, but over that five year span he used that money to help him build FUBU. I said that to say, I'm not going to let someone tell me how to be an entrepreneur when the truth is they probably don't make as much money as I make in my current job. If a guy worth damn near half a billion says keep your job while you are getting started, I'm going to take his advice over anybody on Twitter.

Everybody makes it so cool to say that they're striking out on their own to follow their dream or start a business. That's cool, but I have experience. I have about a decade in entrepreneurship and over a decade of life since I've graduated college. That's a pretty good window of time to evaluate what works and what doesn't. During that window, I've seen a lot of people start a whole lot of things, and I've seen a whole lot of things fail. At first you might look at yourself and think you should follow someone else's plan or journey, but I think it's important for everybody to run with what makes them comfortable. I build for longevity and putting unfair struggles on myself or my family isn't worth it to me just to be able to say, "I'm an entrepreneur." I'll know the time is right when I can smoothly transition from one to the other.

Over the last ten years or so, we've entered into this culture, especially on Twitter, where people live in this false world. In that world, we listen to people who have no credentials just because they said it was a good idea and they were believable. Their success story is just that—theirs. People listen to that story and think, "All I have to do is quit my job and I'll be good." People want to take someone's once-in-a-lifetime fluke and think that will work for them the exact same way. You have to fall in love with the process because you can go hard at something for ten years and it still doesn't work out. No shade, but look at all the people who rap. Generally, the successful ones have fallen in love with the process.

How important is branding for entrepreneurs and small businesses?

We've made it a joke, but it's actually very true—everybody is a brand now. Even if you aren't selling anything, people often think, "What type of guy is he?" That's why to me it's important to build a brand and stand by it if you are going to have your name and face recognizably attached to it. It's important to be a good, standup person before you even try to sell anything.

Do you think there's a relationship between art and anxiety?

To be a creator, or to even be in a space that is art-driven, you must be open—open to trying things and open to feedback that may not be good. As cliché as it sounds, you really have to give yourself to the art to be productive and to help things happen. I used to wonder why certain things didn't come easy to me. I wondered why I had to work extra hard at things that came natural to other people. The older I got, I realized that I had to be present and make myself learn certain skills because in a lot of ways, my anxiety forced me to be knowledgeable. Because of the way it manifests, it required me to develop certain skills so I could do things comfortably and feel good about the end product. It really forces you to have really high standards and the truth is, that can be a good and bad thing.

You said not feeling "classically" trained used to make you feel small and make you shrink. Can you speak more about that?

It's kind of hard to explain because the trend now is so free and flexible. Today, we are given the latitude to do so many things that are unconventional. What I mean by that is anybody can start a podcast or be a chef or whatever. Whereas, when I was coming up, the thinking was a little more traditional—you were a politician, teacher, or carpenter and that was the one thing you did; that was deemed as your thing. For a long time, I felt like I didn't have a "thing," so I felt like something was wrong with me. Like how basketball was Jordan's thing, I never felt that way about anything. One day I made the decision that I'm not going to feel like this for the rest of my life, and I decided I had to start trying my hand at stuff outside of my comfort zone. Sometimes you have to get out there and start exploring; you never know what's going to stick.

You mentioned that you beat yourself up a lot. In your words, "It's hard to beat me down because you are probably late to the party." Do you think that feeling is a product of anxiety?

Yeah, it is. Before I found out what it was and why I felt the way I did, I used to feel like I was the only person who felt like this. That's exactly what it feels like, or that feeling is one way it can manifest itself. You will think you need to be prepared for the worst to happen in every situation, and in the process of making sure you are prepared for everything that can go wrong, you use a lot of energy. That energy could be put towards making things happen correctly, or even better, you could just imagine things will go correctly. Your mindset has to change. I still struggle with it, but readjusting my mindset every so often helps me to overcome these feelings.

When did you have a mindset change towards entrepreneurship and anxiety?

You know we come from a culture that's conservative in a lot of ways. When I was about to go all in as a realtor, I had a lot of people saying, "You might want to get something a little more steady." It put me in a space where I had to look at myself and see that conflict. My nature wanted to go for it. I was only making pennies at my job, and I felt like I wanted to go all in, but I didn't. It was a learning experience for me. When you become a man, you have to learn how to make decisions and stand on them. I say this intentionally; if you're going to take the chance at being successful you have to take that chance. It's one thing to have a job and to be able to pay your bills. That's cool, but for me that's not living. Sometimes you have to force yourself into a place that's not comfortable, and you have to be comfortable with the uncomfortable. It's trial and error, because you've never been here before—but that's where you really shake things up. But like I said, it was a learning experience. I listened to everyone else over myself—and that's not to say they were hating on me—it was just learning that I'm different and what I want is different.

What advice do you have for people trying to overcome anxiety?

I think people really have to dial in to themselves and understand what their strengths and weaknesses are. Make sure you're not following somebody else's goals and ambitions, and for young people that's easy to do. It's easy to look up to or follow someone and try to fill their shoes. What's important is that you feel your own way through your process and do what you feel guided to do. Just like we talked about, society will tell you to risk it all to become an entrepreneur. I can't stress it enough—everyone's path is different and you have to be true to yourself.

This sounds bad, but the one thing that really helps me is understanding that people aren't that smart. That doesn't make you arrogant or better than anyone, but it's a fact. I gave people way too much credit in the past. One of my favorite artists, Andre 3000, said it best, "'Genius' and 'friend' are the most overused words." I had to understand that I can and must think on my own. Realizing that I'm a pretty good thinker gave me so much more confidence. Once you start believing that, you'll stop giving up just because you were met with some opposition or a hurdle. This last part may not be true for everyone, but it's true for me. A lot of the time I thought the only way I did something right was if I did it perfectly, with no challenge or resistance. I thought if something went wrong, it was a failure. That's a bad way of looking at it. Success isn't some quick place you get to. People have to understand that you can have success early on and still fall apart in the end.

> "Instead of worrying about what you cannot control, shift your energy to what you can create." **—Roy Bennett**

Why is understanding pace important?

Some people like to grow fast and don't care if they fall off. I'm obsessed with consistency. If I build something, I want to be able to build it again. I don't worry about being the biggest in my field—that's a lesson I learned from some of my favorite artists. A lot of my favorite artists never tried to be the biggest, but they made it a point to be consistent. Being consistent over a span of 20 years got them a really loyal fanbase. I decided early on that I'd rather be the person that is the most consistent instead of the person that is the hottest but can't do it again. To me, that's the scariest thing—being able to do something once and not being able to do it again.

What advice would you give a new designer or someone who wants to get into the apparel game?

Move slowly and intentionally. It's easy to go belly up in this line of work. This is where my accounting mind and experience comes into play. I understand inventory and expenses. I'm always trying to compile data to make the right decisions. Take something as simple as sizes: you have to produce an optimal amount of each. It's easy to say "I'll go print 50 t-shirts," but you should consult your data to understand what sizes you sell most. If you don't, you'll have 50 shirts that you have already paid for, but you won't have the correct sizes. Without the correct sizes, you'll be sitting on those shirts not making any money. Always remember, it's easy to get people to buy something once—especially t-shirts—but it's hard to recreate that sale. You gotta build and position your brand in a way that people will want to come back and shop again.

What does resilience mean to you?

Resilience is knowing and understanding how long to fight. To me, it means fighting until there is no way to win—some people would say to the death. But to me, it's whatever you feel is a winnable circumstance or your best way out.

What's more important for success: passion or skill?

Passion. Skill is what you have to build. There's a difference in skill and talent. A talent is picking up a baseball the first time and hitting a homerun. Skill is learning how to hit a single every time, and learning how to place the baseball. In my opinion, passion leads to building skill. People can be talented, but don't have the work ethic or the drive to make it happen so the talent doesn't take them anywhere. But as long as you have the passion, you'll find a way to improve and make your talent come through.

> "Failure is only wasted if you can't figure out why." **—Rev. Dr. Conway Edwards,** One Community Church, Plano, TX

CHAPTER 4

EMBRACING FAILURE

Jordan B. Franklin, Esq.

Instagram & Twitter: @jovant_garde

"Continue moving forward, shaping your future, and never give up."

After failing the bar exam for the second time, Jordan Franklin's mom said to her, "Say the poem." The poem was *Invictus* by William Ernest Henley, which ends with the famous words, "I am the master of my fate; I am the captain of my soul."

In Latin, invictus means unconquerable, and that word describes Jordan perfectly. Did you know it costs roughly $575 to take the bar exam and that there is a 4-month waiting period to receive your results? How about that "bar exam suicides" are very common amongst recent law grads? Can you imagine receiving the dreaded "unfortunately" letter after committing yourself to studying 12 hours a day for two months? When you give 100% of yourself to anything, it's hard not to look at yourself as a failure when you fail.

With that context in mind, let's investigate the journey of Jordan Franklin, a trademark attorney from Houston, TX. Throughout my interview with Jordan, or "Jo" as her friends call her, she provided valuable information for dreamers, influencers, and entrepreneurs. So, let's jump right into it. Who is Jordan Franklin?

Jo is a Houston native with a natural gift for persevering and helping others. She's an analytical person by nature, always looking and searching for the "why" in any given situation. Calling her meticulous would be an understatement—we are talking about someone who stores her rejection letters for motivation. She attended Baylor University as a Biology/Pre-Med major where she initially dreamt of becoming a reconstructive surgeon. She would volunteer her services to repair the cleft lips of less fortunate children, but that dream was derailed. She realized it wasn't her true calling while taking college chemistry, where she couldn't shake the thought, "God, this can't be what you have planned for me, because I'm over this."

But something happened during this time that would change the course of her life. She noticed how much she enjoyed debating the "affirmative" against the "negative" in her philosophy and political science class, so she decided to change her major. She eventually graduated from Baylor with a B.A. in Philosophy and a minor in Religion. Before jumping right into law school, she decided to get some hands-on experience to verify that this was the career for her. "It didn't take me long to realize that this is what God had for me," she said. Eager to start the process, she began applying to law schools. But before being granted her first "yes," she piled up a stack of rejection letters.

"I think I applied to 17 programs," she recalled. "If it wasn't for my pastors, I probably would've let it go."

Her pastor urged her to give it one last shot and she did. She was ultimately accepted into an HBCU with a very rich history. One interesting fact is that she chose a Historically Black College/University because in her words, "I needed an HBCU experience." It was a harsh reality to be informed that there are only six HBCU law schools left, due to many of our law schools getting closed down and losing accreditation at an alarming rate. The only HBCU law programs that remain are: Texas Southern University, Howard University, Florida A&M University, North Carolina Central University, The University of the District of Columbia, and Jordan's alma mater "Thee Southern University."

With Black women only making up 1.8% of all attorneys, it makes sense why Jo "needed" that experience. Although she chose an HBCU, her take on Baylor was quite interesting. To put it bluntly, "I appreciate my time at Baylor because it taught me to maneuver as part of that 1.8%." Statistically, Baylor is about 2% Black, including the athletes.

Although it didn't seem like it at the time, her rejection and learning how to navigate was preparing her for arguably the most trying time of her life. After graduating with her J.D., Jo was ready to venture out and take on the bar exam. But a harsh reality would soon follow. For two months, Jo was up around 6 AM to head to the library and study; at times not returning until well into the night. So imagine her surprise when she got a call from her friend asking if she was ok. Confused, Jo asked her, "Why wouldn't I be?"

What Jo didn't realize is that the "pass list" for the bar exam had been posted and her name was absent. When Jo went to take the bar exam for the first time she was filled with confidence. "You couldn't have told me I was going to fail," she said.

The confidence seemed warranted, considering how she studied for hours on end and had never failed a single exam in law school. "The bar exam kicked my ass mentally and spiritually," she admitted.

After receiving the news, she screamed, questioned if God was upset with her, and went through a depression before attempting the bar for a second time—something she was advised against. People she respected would tell her, "You need to give yourself time to process this and put your plan together."

When you leave it all on the field, it's hard to accept defeat. To be clear on what she was up against, let me paint the picture of the bar. The bar varies from state to state, making it extremely difficult to develop a consistent study plan. This is a 15-hour exam that takes place over the course of three days, and days one and three are pure writing. Exam takers are expected to type law from memory, which means that in order to be successful, you must become so familiar with the law that it's essentially second nature. She said that after not passing it the first time, "I felt like a failure. I'm like the rock of the family and I didn't want anyone to see me in that moment. I pushed everyone away."

But after this hard-fought battle with depression and anxiety, she went against her own better judgement and she took it again—just 5 months after failing it for the first time. Although she failed again, she felt eerily confident about taking it for the third time. This go-around, she would take her time to thoroughly prepare. "I'm a detailed person," she explained. "I [usually] keep my ducks in a row, but I let one of my ducks get out of line."

Although her emotions had gotten the best of her during her previous attempts, this time she would use the period to prepare a plan to put her in the best position to pass. She thought back to and found hope in the fact that she only failed by nine measly points. "I have always been a good student, but I have horrible test anxiety," she explained. "Still, once I get my nerves in check I'm usually good. I may not be the smartest in the room, but you won't outwork me."

In Texas, you need a 675 to pass the bar. On her third attempt, Jo passed by scoring well into the 700s, proving that with a little effort and persistence, one can achieve great things.

Jo was the perfect person for this chapter because of her transparency about her story. Jo is a product of faith, resilience, and the trials (no pun intended) she overcame. So now that we know who she is, let's talk about her passion and what you need to know.

Jo has a passion for law because it keeps her sharp and she enjoys advocating for people. During her second year of law school, she realized that the trademark arena is where she would focus her skills. Knowing she wanted to work with creatives and entertainers, she asked herself, "What area best fits their needs?" Trademark law is an area that is unclear—but vitally important—to many creatives, so I met up with Jo at Kaffeine Coffee in Houston's 3rd Ward to discuss it with her. Along the way, we touched on dealing with adversity, her path to becoming a trademark attorney, and most importantly, overcoming failure.

The interview that follows is truly thought-provoking and will leave you eager to turn to the next page of your story.

What is intellectual property and how do you protect it?

It's funny, because intellectual property is literally what it sounds like. To put it into legal terms, it is the protection of the tangible expression of your ideas. This means that those protections don't kick in until the idea becomes something you can conceptualize or build. Intellectual property is an umbrella term, and there are three main properties: patents, copyrights, and trademarks.

Patents—These protect inventions because you can't patent ideas. The idea must become something tangible, because depending on the patent, you must submit a blueprint for what the item is and how it works. Patents are for your inventions; the things you build and create.

Copyrights—These are used to protect artistic expression. Think films, music, photography, paintings, and sculptures. Basically, works of art. But still, the idea must be pulled out of your head first, and at that point, a copyright can be introduced. I explain it like this: you can be a photographer and have this beautiful shot in your head, but until you have taken the picture you can't copyright it. However once you've pressed the shutter, copyright protection can be introduced.

Trademarks—A trademark is essentially what a consumer or a consumer base can identify you with. They then correlate that identification with whatever good or service you provide or whatever industry you are in.

Does a brand need a trademark? If so, at what point should they get one?

Absolutely. Especially if you are building any type of business or legacy. It's your branding, it's how people identify you and what you do, and it could be the very thing that sets you apart.

Regarding the question of how long you should wait—not too long. I've seen instances where people put it off and can't get the trademark protections because somebody already has something similar.

You don't have to be well-established, but it's something you should be thinking about in the beginning. I would consider trademarking around the same time you are deciding what type of business entity you'll be forming (i.e. LLC, S-Corp, B-Corp). In those early stages you should start asking yourself, "What am I getting trademarked?" Whether it's just your name or your first logo, that's a good time to start the process.

I think brands should realize that, as you grow, your branding grows as well. Legally we call that your "trademark portfolio," and every major brand has one. That portfolio basically encompasses every single trademark that you own—even the ones you don't use anymore but want to prevent someone else from capitalizing on. Your trademark portfolio won't start with 50 varieties, it's something you'll grow into.

The most common example I use is Nike. Nike's very first trademark application, which was filed sometime in the 1960s, was just for the name, and they only filed it under one trademark class: athletic uniforms. Fast forward to the present, and they own every single variation of their logo, ranging from the iconic Swoosh to the slogan "Just do it."

They also have trademarks of Nike in various different fonts and languages, and even the shoe names—from Air Max to Air Jordan—are all included in their trademark portfolio. Over the decades, Nike grew into the mega corporation that it is now, and I think it's important for brands to realize that your trademarking is something that will continue to grow as your business and brand grows.

How long does a trademark last?

It could last forever if you are actively using it. That said, there are steps that come after the initial filing that you should be aware of. For instance, five years after your initial filing you have to submit renewal documents which are basically saying, "Hey, we are still using this trademark." Then, every ten years after that, you do the same thing. So that's essentially how a trademark can go on forever, but I'd highly recommend reaching out to a professional to help you get things started.

One quick tip: I always tell people to list their business as the owner of the trademark and not themselves. Here's why: business property and trademarks are considered "property," and ownership of them all can be passed down to your heirs after your death. Kobe Bryant is an unfortunate, but great example of this. Before he passed, his company filed for 12 trademarks, including one for his daughter's nickname, "Mambacita." Because he filed for these trademarks under his company name, his heirs will inherit the rights to those trademarks. They can continue to live on and produce from them even in Kobe's absence. That's why stuff like that is important, because if it's something you've already monetized, that wealth can be passed down and continue to live on.

What is more important for success: passion or skill?

Passion all day. I can't speak on other industries, but in the legal field, you must have passion. It helps you go the extra mile when things aren't looking good. The last thing you want is an attorney representing you who isn't passionate, because that shows in their work. It's not just law, people usually take what they are passionate about and build on that. That's what takes you to the next level in law and in life.

What's a useful piece of advice you would like to share?

Embrace your failures. Although it's hard to see it initially, they make you better. Secondly, don't focus so much on results that you forget the process. The process is your foundation. When building anything, if you cut corners, the foundation of the final product will be weak.

One of my favorite analogies comes from this devotional that I really enjoy. In short, when silver is being formed, it's put through fire to remove the impurities. Silversmiths know their weapon is ready when they can see their reflection in it, but that readiness requires the silver going through some serious fire before it's perfect and sharp enough.

Implement that in your life—realize that you have to go through some fire before you are ready. As hard as that process is, you have to embrace it because it's only making you stronger.

In a separate conversation, you said that God's grace and mercy helped push you through your failure. Could you explain?

Sure. At the time, I allowed not passing the bar exam to completely shatter not just my personal confidence but my spiritual confidence as well. I felt like, even in that uncertainty, God was gracious with me and continued to bless and push me. Because of that journey, I am able to be where I am now and do the things I've done and plan to do.

Do you think people focus too much on appearing to be successful instead of actually working towards success?

I won't necessarily say people focus too much on appearing to be successful. I think the biggest mistake people make is not being transparent in their successes. Many successful people just paint the picture alluding to the process of success being easy. Whereas, I think the most important part of success is documenting and being transparent about the process of getting there. That's why I am always open about my failures. Not only do they add to your story, but they make the success sweeter and also more attainable for your audience.

People have to know that perfection is non-existent. We owe it to the people coming behind us to be as honest as possible about the steps, the missteps, and the failures. We have to be honest about everything that we encountered on our journey to success.

Is there a right time to give up and stop trying?

I don't ever believe in giving up on a dream, honestly. I feel that if you are dreaming it, if you can't get the vision out of your mind, then it was placed there for a reason. It's your duty to understand it and help it find its intended purpose. So I say never give up on your dreams. To me, if you focus your mind, effort, and energy on it, it will happen.

You mentioned having a tougher road as a woman in law. What advice do you have for the women—especially Black women—coming behind you?

My biggest piece of advice to women of color in this industry, and specifically Black women, is to have a support group.

And if that's a Black woman who practices in a different area of law, even better. Black women, especially Black women in law, experience situations that are unique to us as a race and gender. We only make up less than 2% of the legal field, so we have to provide support to each other. That support will prove helpful in navigating what it looks like to be one of us in this industry. Build a solid network and lean on them, even if it's just to go get drinks and chop it up. Just be sure to have an outlet that understands your experiences. That's a big thing, and it's a huge way to stay sane because this industry is already stressful enough. Make it fun, socialize, and build sisterhood.

In our interview you talked about going through a minor depression after failing the bar. Can you talk about how you got through it?

I got through that depression with my faith. I know I talk about that a lot, but it's the truth. When I was going into the exam for the third time, I wanted to completely change the way I approached it mentally and spiritually. So I did things that I hadn't done before. One of my good friends, who is a worship leader at our church, always says, "In order to see things that you have not seen, you have to do things that you have not done."

So for me that rang pretty true and I started approaching things differently—for example, the way I approached prayer. Sometimes I would get a little distracted in my meditation, so I started trying to make sure that the time I was allotting was an uninterrupted time that was dedicated completely to God.

I also fasted for the first time, and it was so powerful that I started fasting more. Honestly, it was just things like that that pulled me out of it.

What should people ask themselves after failure? What did you ask yourself?

I think the biggest thing to ask yourself after failure is how bad do you want whatever it is you are seeking to achieve. Because if whatever it is that you're working towards means that much to you, you won't allow anything to stand in your way of getting it.

> "There is only one thing that makes a dream impossible to achieve: the fear of failure." —**Paulo Coelho**

How do you define success?

I believe success has a very subjective definition. For me, success is equal to purpose. I feel that the more I walk in my purpose and align myself with that purpose, the more successful I am. So to me, success equals walking in and fulfilling your purpose. Walking in your purpose may not always result in wealth, but that's because I don't think success always equals wealth. I think success means fulfillment in my personal experience. Success is more about personal fulfilment than wealth.

What did you learn about yourself when bouncing back or going through your failure?

I think the biggest thing that I learned bouncing back from that failure is that I'm stronger than I give myself credit for. Sometimes I get in my own way, which allows self-doubt to creep in and cause confidence issues. Being able to overcome that made me stronger. I started to believe that if I was able to overcome that, there's nothing that I can't overcome again.

Any final advice for the readers of this chapter?

I think the biggest thing to help a reader is to understand that if you have survived before, you can survive again. In one of my lowest moments, I couldn't see the forest for the trees—but I learned that the forest is where things really grow. That perspective shift has helped me a lot.

> "The secret of happiness, you see, is not found in seeking more, but in developing the capacity to enjoy less." **–Socrates**

CHAPTER 5

LIVE SIMPLY

Kayland "KP" Partee

Instagram: @k.partee | @dirtynapkins

"Don't rush the process. Things will happen at the perfect time."

One of my favorite books is *The Art of Living* by Epictetus. Epictetus was a Greek philosopher who believed that the key to true happiness was mastering yourself. *The Art of Living* is truly worth reading if you are interested in some insightful commentary around living a fulfilling life and being a good person.

I know you're thinking, "What does Greek philosophy have to do with this specific chapter?" My answer is simple—everything. There is a philosophical idea in *The Art of Living* that really changed my approach to life: "Live simply for your own sake." In that passage, the line that really gave me life was the following: "The first task of the person who wishes to live wisely is to free himself or herself from the confines of self-absorption."

As I mentioned earlier, in a lot of ways *Dream* is an imaginary line that will always lead me home; and by home, I mean a clear and calm mental space. As I was contemplating who best fit this chapter's needs, the stars somewhat aligned. I thought, "Who embodies the quality of simplicity or "living simply?" I needed to look no further than my childhood friend Kayland Partee, or "KP" as his clients call him. KP and I have been friends for as long as I can remember, but we reconnected sometime around 2016.

KP is a wedding photographer by trade, but I would be doing him a major disservice if I stopped there. He also does video work ranging from wedding videos to commercials, and his client list ranges from the local smoothie shop to the local Mercedes dealership. He is also a part owner of a country club, but it is his most recent venture that brought the two of us back together.

He is the owner and creator of a startup streaming network called Rewind TV. The goal is to grow this platform into a streaming juggernaut that will one day rival the likes of Hulu, Netflix, and HBO Max. On the surface, it would be hard to believe that someone who has his hands in this many fires could be the ideal spokesperson for living a simple life. But in reality, KP's simple approach to life is something he has had since we were kids.

I remember one time KP and I skipped a day in high school. Me being overly excited, I thought we were about to do some reckless teenage things. I soon found KP had something a lot simpler in mind. We drove around the city and talked about life for a while before we stopped at American Deli in Metrocenter Mall and got several orders of wings, a couple sides of fries, and two large drinks. After we finished, we went to Jackson State's

Homecoming pep rally on the Gibbs-Green Memorial Plaza, at which point we found some open space in the "horseshoe" (Jackson State Alumni would understand this) and watched the band and admired college women until it was time for Kayland to head to basketball practice.

KP has maintained his same simple spirit all these years later, thus making him the perfect person for this chapter.

Before COVID-19 shut down most travel, KP ran an Airbnb in New Orleans which he invited me to come visit. I decided to take him up on that offer, and I planned a trip to New Orleans to get a new feel for the city. During that trip, Kayland became the first person I interviewed for this book and he gave me the encouragement to harness and hone my talent.

I booked this trip because before now, I had been to New Orleans twice and I told KP I had no intentions of going back. Being the salesman that he is, he convinced me to give it another shot. Because of him I have a new found love for the Big Easy.

It's 3:26 pm on a Thursday and the airport had a vibe similar to that of Memorial Day weekend in Vegas (pre-COVID, of course). The people were lost in the moment and seemed to not really care about time. Instantly, my guard was lowered and without my consent, the city was about to take me on an easy ride for the weekend. The writing on the wall should have been clear after a round of tequila shots with a bride-to-be, sailboat mechanic, and a shady lawyer —think Saul from *Breaking Bad*.

Before now, NOLA had never quite lived up to the hype for me. When I thought of New Orleans, I thought old, drab, and lifeless. However, this time my experience was delightfully different. All the credit is due to KP who went out of his way to make sure I got a true New Orleans experience. In his words "I wouldn't dare take you to Bourbon."

KP picked me up from the airport, but called and asked that I grab him a daiquiri to-go. Not knowing the culture of the city, I ignorantly said, "They are not going to let me carry a daiquiri out of the airport, man."

He replied with a simple, "Yes they will—this isn't Dallas bro." Without any hesitation the waitress whipped up the drink, threw a top on it, and I politely asked her to add another. She patiently mixed another and sent me on my way.

I mentioned that we've been friends for quite some time, and let me tell you—when KP is confident about something, you'll know. He's a great salesman and he loves to drive his point home when he's right. As we left the airport, he looked at me and said, "We chillin? I don't have any shoots planned. Let's hangout." His idea of hanging out was enjoying a meal at Emeril Lagasse's restaurant, Meril, followed by a stop to grab a bottle of sangria from Lola's, and then heading to the French Market to walk, talk, and snap a few photos of the scenery. Afterward, we enjoyed some beignets from Café Du Monde and I quickly discovered KP's new found love of trying out restaurants. Mind you, this was all within the first couple of hours that KP scooped me from the airport.

Fast forward to interview day where KP said, "I want to show you around before we get started." Three more restaurants, countless drinks, and the best alligator sausage later, I was more worried about dancing than interviewing. This sums up the joy he finds in the simplest things.

"I tell people all the time, in an alternate universe I would just be a tour guide in New Orleans," he said.

Although the food and the energy was great, I was most impressed by the culture of the city. I was lucky enough to talk to people who have never left, and all I can say is New Orleans is a resilient city and if it's one thing that contributes to the culture, it's the no worries attitude. That attitude fits KP almost perfectly.

Although in another life he dreams of being a tour guide in New Orleans, KP is presently an up-and-coming television producer. The second part of this interview took place as we wrapped up season one of our new show, *Dirty Napkins*. The premise of the show is to have a conversation with your favorite people in some of your favorite restaurants. As we celebrated our accomplishment, we drank and ate good food as we reflected on how we got here.

A big part of that reflection was centered around the conversation of ownership. To give Kayland his proper credit, he takes ownership to the next level. He uses his own money to fund his dreams, and specifically, his new network. His reason is all you need to know to understand who KP is at the core.

"I just want to showcase the talents we have to offer—my talents, my friends' talents, and the city's talents," he said. "Instead of going out and looking for investors, I just asked, 'Why can't we make our own show and do our own network?'"

He sees it as a natural fit. He gets to produce and direct content in a way that's true to him, all while doing his favorite pastime—day drinking and checking out new eateries.

Both interviews took place in two very relaxing environments. In New Orleans, as we finally slowed down, we took the ferry to Algiers Point to talk and to get a good view of the city. In Jackson, we sat at his studio drinking tequila and wine with no one present but the immediate team. All this is a testament to KP's mantra, which is trusting the process and being patient. As KP put it, "Don't rush the process; things will happen at the perfect time and remember that patience is a virtue."

"These days, everyone wants it, 'now, now, now,'" he continued.

He believes that no matter what you are doing, you should seek to patiently master something rather than trying to be "ok" at everything. KP closes with the old cliché saying, "The race isn't always won by the swiftest."

Enjoy this excerpt from my interview with my friend, and hopefully long time producer, KP.

How do you define success?

I know a lot of people value success in monetary goals. I used to define success in terms of followers and money. Now I feel if you are happy with what you are doing, you are successful. Money is nice, but that isn't what makes me happy. Now, putting out a quality product that people thoroughly enjoy makes me happy. Me and the team thought about the project and put it into action. Once it's out for the world to see, I'm happy. That embodies success to me.

There are so many people who think of stuff, but never do it. They have all these ideas that never materialize. Bringing our content to people's TV, iPhone, Facebook, or Instagram is a win to me. I had to learn to be comfortable where I am and with what I have in life. There are a lot of people who wish they had the things and talents I have. The same way people may look at you and think, "Man, Taylor is writing; I wish I could write." You just have to take one of your strengths or build a new skill and get to work.

Staying humble helps me keep things simple. I don't consider myself a big time photographer or videographer, it helps me see the small successes better. So my advice is this: take a step back, slow down, and enjoy where you are because a lot of people wish they could get there.

One last thing about money and material things. There are plenty of people who make tons of money, but are miserable at their job and hate what they do for a living. If it's always about money or followers; if it's always, "I won't be successful until I get here," or "I need this many followers before I start my business," you'll never be successful. You are always going to want something you don't have. My happiest days come from just riding my bicycle down Esplanade Avenue in NOLA with a drink in my hand. Gotta enjoy each moment.

Why is ownership so important to you?

I've always felt that if you don't have to work for someone, dont. If you work for other people they are really in the position to tell you what you can and can't do and exactly how they want it. For me, it's about creating my own streaming network where we can use our own creative abilities to showcase our talents and our city's talents. I feel like we can start with our local talent and let it grow from there. Everyone had to start somewhere, including all the top online platforms.

I just want to showcase all of these cool stories and different backgrounds. But I also started Rewind TV to show people who may want to do something similar to just go for it. I just wanted to show people it's never too late to start your own business. If you have a dream, shoot for it. Whether it's entrepreneurship, attaining a certain job, or even getting back in school, go for it.

What are your thoughts on starting a business in your hometown versus moving away?

The positive thing about being an entrepreneur in my hometown of Jackson, MS is that people tend to support you if you support yourself. It's give and take. The thing is you have to support yourself and do good business.

You will always hear negative comments like, "My city is too small." People always told me I should move to Atlanta, LA, or Dallas. They would say, "Man if you moved to LA you would be on, you would be making a lot more." Those people who told me to move may have been right, I might have booked $10-20K shoots if I moved, but I'm comfortable in my own city. I always tell people that there is plenty of money right here in Jackson, and there is opportunity here too.

Opportunity is the biggest thing for entrepreneurs. You can move to a bigger market and create a business, but if there are twice as many people doing that same business, that's counterproductive. Now you are fighting to be seen in some new city, versus back home all you have to do is create a business and market it to the right people. Your work ethic and hustle will stand out and people will already know you.

Why is living simply important to you?

That's just how I like to live my life. At the end of the day life is short, and we can live our life worrying and stressing about how to get a million dollars, but is it worth your peace of mind? I just appreciate the little things, that's where I find happiness. That's also where I find the mental space and time to start all these new business ventures. I can't stress it enough—I appreciate the little things. When we started *Dirty Napkins*, I appreciated us doing just one episode. So the fact that we completed two seasons is a blessing. If you appreciate the small things, the big things will feel even better.

Why is it important to trust the process?

I have always been a fan of enjoying the process, from when I played sports to starting Partee Photography and Partee Films. When you embrace the process, you can look back and enjoy the come up. In a lot of ways I had somewhat of a lucky start early in my career—I worked with the Southern University Dancing Dolls and did a few high-profile sweet sixteen parties and weddings. Every opportunity was different, but the process of each made the end result so worth it.

My very first photoshoot was in my living room, with some beginner lights. When I was starting out, I used to do all my shoots at my house. Now, I'm in a two story studio downtown. It makes you appreciate it more when you remember and look back on where you came from.

Not only do you have to trust the process with everything you do, you also have to see it and you have to believe it. I couldn't have pitched *Dirty Napkins* to you if I didn't believe in it first. You have to be the main person pushing your cause or idea; you have to be the one saying, "We have to do this!" People will see your energy and how serious you are and will want to get onboard to help.

> "Most people want to skip the process, not knowing that when you skip steps, you miss lessons. If you start small and build on what you have, you can continue to multiply that into something greater while picking up all of the valuable lessons along the way." **—Nipsey Hussle**

On the journey to achieving your dream, which is more important: passion or skill?

You need a little bit of both, but I'm going to say passion. You can be passionate about something and not be talented at it. On the flip side, even the most talented person needs passion. If your heart isn't in your work, you're probably going to deliver subpar results. I'll use myself as an example. When I started out, there were a lot of photographers who had been in the business longer than me. People started hiring me because they saw how passionate I was about my work. People can see your passion; they can tell if you really care about what you're doing. Your level of passion is always going to show in the work. I think simply caring about what you do goes a long way.

What's something you think every Black person should do?

I think every Black person should go to Essence Fest at least once. It's so much Black pride, entrepreneurship, and excellence in one place. If you want to start a business, that's a good place to start. It just feels like everyone there wants to see Black people win.

Any last words of advice?

Stay humble, and live simply.

> "You can borrow knowledge, but not action." **–James Clear**

CHAPTER 6

MAKE YOUR OWN LANE

Matt "Yayo the Drummer" Mayberry

Instagram: @yayo_thedrummer

"The best knowledge gained is knowledge shared." –Booker T Washington

When something feels right but you aren't quite sure how to attain it, consider this: make your own lane. Let's say you are an artist who just can't seem to find the spotlight that you believe you deserve. Instead of harping on that, put the work in and make them notice you. Meet my good friend Matthew, who goes by (and I'm not kidding) Matt, Yayo, Champagne, Mayberry and the "One Man Band," to name a few. But for the sake of simplicity, let's go with Matt.

This interview was important to me because he possesses a quality that I believe we all need: drive. Don't get me wrong, all the guests in this book are driven; but after I finish this chapter you will understand even more why Matt is the poster child when it comes to drive and making your own lane.

Matt was born and raised in Jackson, MS, and he has always been a "class clown" of sorts—a fact that was verified by multiple people. Here's the thing: throughout this piece you might come across a story that makes you question its authenticity, but I'm here to tell you that every—and I do mean *every*—story in this piece has been verified.

Matt won't admit it, but he is a phenomenal storyteller. Another thing you have to understand about Matt before we continue is that he is always on the go. In order to get this interview done, I basically spent an entire day with him. We started early in the morning with a tequila sunrise as he tinted a car, then we stopped by his garden, followed by a brief visit to church before ending with a game of Uno while having a nightcap of wine.

With no hesitation, Matt agreed to my request to verify the stories he would share with me and he immediately came up with the idea that we should FaceTime people to answer any questions I may have. So it began, I arrived at Matt's house around 8 am, and in true fashion, he was up and active as he is every time you encounter him. I started unpacking my bag and telling him how the interview was going to go. And as I started to explain my goals for the day, he received a FaceTime call. "I'm pullin up, where do you want me to park?" I heard the person on the other side of the screen say.

Matt looked at me and said, "I got a car to tint. Come over here; we can still talk." I learned that day that one of his first hustles was tinting cars at a detail shop. After realizing the cash he could make from that, he consistently started to hustle harder. "Window tinting changed my life," he explained. "It showed me that you could get real money by doing things other than becoming a doctor or a lawyer."

Matt believes that every black and brown person should have a trade. In his words, "Trades build human capital. The goal is to make yourself more diverse." To be clear, he isn't advocating for or against going to college; he is simply encouraging people to seek education in any form.

As we were closing up our conversation about trades, he received another FaceTime call. This would be my first testimony of the day. He immediately paused the tint job, slipped his tinting tools into his apron, and gave our soon to be first guest a quick rundown. He handed me the phone before he returned to tinting and said, "Ask her whatever."

The first thing I see is a woman in a t-shirt with the words "Black AF" on it, which was ironic because the interview happened to take place on Juneteenth. The details of the conversation aren't important; just understand this is how the majority of the conversations took place. We spoke about her experience meeting "Yayo," and she summed it up in this way: "It's always a moment or a movie."

As Matt was wrapping up the tint job, he poured me a glass of wine and I asked, "So if tinting was your first baby, how did you get into drums?"

"It was really my pops," he answered. "They called him 'maestro.' But my family, including my brother, played a huge part."

Prior to our interview, I did some research on Matt and found a common theme. Everybody I talked to in my early research mentioned some story of Matt and drums. One person even recalled a memory of Matt playing congas around the school as early as the 4th grade.

"I've been playing drums for a minute," Matt humbly mentioned.

"Well when did you see it really take a turn?" I replied.

His answer was "college," but before we could go any further, he told me he had an errand to run. I loaded up my bag and the adventure continued. We rode around the city to take a few pics for his One Man Band apparel line, but somehow we ended up at a garden deep in the country.

We got out of the car and I asked, "So what's here?"

"I've had a garden since at least my sophomore year in high school," he explained. "A garden will teach you patience and that God is real. Just look at how something so small can turn into something that can nurture, heal, and feed us."

The conversation took an interesting turn when he intertwined George Washington Carver while continuing to enlighten me on gardening. I soon realized that Carver and Dr. Booker T. Washington had carved a special place in Matt's heart, due in no small part to the fact that he is a proud alumnus of Tuskegee University in Alabama, where both men taught. Tuskegee has a rich history and tradition that can rival any HBCU. Founded in a one-room shack in 1881, the Tuskegee Institute was headed by Booker T. Washington who served as the school's president until his death in 1915. One of the most enlightening quotes of this piece comes from the genius who is Booker T. Washington: "The best knowledge gained is knowledge shared."

To this day, nearly 75% of minority veterinarians still come from Tuskegee, which is fitting because Matt majored in Animal Science. After some additional thought he added a concentration in Plant and Soil Science because of his interest in gardening. He finished with a B.S. in Animal, Poultry and Veterinary Science with a minor in Business. While enlisted in the Army, he then went on to receive two MBA degrees, and become a medical services officer.

Make Your Own Lane

However, throughout all of this, it's his continued focus on drumming that speaks volumes to the importance of maintaining a hustle, drive, and making your own lane. Matt was in the marching band at Tuskegee, but various people report that he spent more time drumming at an "old people blues bar" in Tuskegee on the weekend.

"I just looked at it like I was bettering myself and building my skills," he recounted. "None of the students were coming because it was too far outside of the city." He credits that experience with teaching him how to make the most out of any crowd. The story was truly fascinating, but of course I couldn't believe it that easily.

He looked at me and said, "Oh yea, you want to verify all of this stuff." He then made more FaceTime calls to several more people and handed me the phone to talk to these individuals each time.

According to multiple sources, he started these "Drummer DJ" parties during his college days going back as far as 2007. The first source said, "I met Matt sophomore year. He has always been high energy. He can blend in anywhere like a chameleon; he's hella adaptable."

Another gentleman told me about the crazy parties that took place during those times. "Man, he used to have house parties in college where he would have the drum set in the living room and he would control the crowd and the party with his iPod and his drum set."

The next person I spoke with further confirmed this anecdote. "His house parties were crazy. He had hookah before it was a thing. His parties were drums, hookahs, and ho*'s."

The most powerful statement of the day was given by someone who works heavily in the entertainment industry, but chose to remain anonymous. "He is probably the most electrifying person you'll ever meet. I think he was Yayo before he became Yayo The Drummer."

With his momentum high, Matt decided to take his Drummer DJ parties on the road. One year at a Jackson State University Homecoming celebration, he played an event that would put him in touch with some people who would push him to explore his concept in Dallas, TX. Little did I know that all of that experience and exploring this concept in Dallas would allow me and my old friend Yayo to reconnect.

Although we graduated from the same high school (Callaway High), he was gone before I transferred in. However, I had a new car and I was in search of some tint. When I went to a local tint shop, the owner referred me to, you guessed it, Matt. From there we didn't stay in touch, but we reconnected through a brief scuffle, of all things. Drinks were involved and friends quickly stepped in to break us up. Anywho, that scuffle led to us reconnecting the next day and staying in touch.

One weekend, I went out to a day party with our mutual friend Careal. When we walked in, I saw Yayo with his shirt off and some gorgeous lady pouring a generous amount of Ciroc in his mouth. All of this was happening while he was simultaneously playing drums to Usher's, "You Don't Have to Call." Fast forward a couple of hours as the party is closing, I asked him, "When are you headed out?" "Now," he replied. "I gotta slide to Houston for a set tomorrow. I'll be back Monday though; I gotta work and we gotta take pictures."

I always surround myself with people I believe are willing to work for what they want. So from that day on, I began taking pictures for Matt's apparel line, One Man Band. From that moment, I knew Matt was driven to achieve his dream—whatever that dream was. That's the hustle it takes and the grind you need to make it all come together.

As we were talking, he got a call from his mom. She asked when he was coming to the church and he said, "I'm at the garden with Lil Jeremy. We are talking and verifying some stories."

"Ok see you soon," she replied, before jokingly adding, "People have to verify your stories."

So we loaded up again and made a brief stop by his church. Due to the coronavirus, he helped to set up the equipment outdoors, stayed for soundcheck, and then we went back to his house where I concluded my initial interview over a few games of Uno and a few glasses of wine.

After years of hustle and maintaining his Drummer DJ sets, he was presented with the opportunity to go on the road with Lil Wayne, who also officially coined him "The One Man Band."

"It all happened so fast," he recalled. "Tez came up to me one day and said, 'Learn these songs, you got rehearsal in a week.'"

The rest has been history. Matt is driven by his work ethic and determination to not be average. I asked who he looks to for inspiration. "Travis Barker," he responded. "He taught me the discipline I needed to instill in myself in order to take my career to a new level."

And he has taken that example to heart. On most days, Matt is up early and getting a workout in to take care of his body. Even during our interview, he took a break to ride his bike to the store to pick up a few items. "Travis taught me that in order to perform at a high level, your stamina has to be right. And also, as a drummer, you have to keep yourself up or people won't take you seriously."

Matt is genuine, fair, and true to himself. As we finished,

his last words were truly inspiring. "How some people can say their cleats took them all around the world, I can say my sticks did that for me; and anyone willing to work can say the same for their craft."

Without further ado, enjoy this interview with my good friend Matt, aka Yayo the Drummer.

What is more important in order to achieve your dreams: passion or skill?

To me, they are one and the same. Of course you have to be skilled, but I don't think one is more important than the other—they need to coexist. If you are passionate about something, you are going to do your best to build your own human capital in it. Human capital is basically skill development and preparation. For instance, let's say you want to start a garden and you want to grow and sell crops. You have to do a lot of studying to become a skilled gardener; it's not as simple as planting a few seeds. I studied soil science in college, so I understand the hard work that being a high level gardener requires. You have to know about stuff like weeds and you have to be knowledgeable about soil, horizons, and more.

That's why I feel they need to coexist. If you are passionate about something, you are going to build your own human capital in whatever it is. You build your capital by taking whatever it is you are passionate about and studying it for your own knowledge, not just because some school or someone is forcing you to. It's like the preparation phase, but to me "passion" exists in the preparation phase. When you care, you are going to prepare yourself for whatever opportunity comes. You need passion because it gets you up and keeps you going when your tank is on E.

You've said before that, "Manifestation is real." Care to explain?

You know I toured with [Lil] Wayne before the world shut down. It's funny, because I was telling people I was doing it before it actually came to fruition. I was manifesting it; I said it was going to happen and it did. That's why I always tell people, manifestation is the truth, and you can manifest anything. If you keep on saying, "I'm going to the league, I'm going to the league," and you keep working and making strides towards it, a door is going to open.

But don't get it twisted—working towards it is just as important. I think the Bible says it best, "Faith without works is dead." Your "works" are equally as important as your "faith." Once you put in that work and the door opens, you have to be ready. If you walk in the door and you aren't ready, you can't fault anyone but yourself. The door was opened for you, so if you fail, it's on you.

That's where preparation and opportunity meet. When my door opened, I had the skill. My preparation plus the opportunity equaled success.

What is the best piece of advice a parent has given you?

It was a Bible verse, Matthew 6:33: "But seek first his kingdom and his righteousness, and all these things will be given to you as well." Basically, it just means to put God first, and all your desires will be given to you. You have to trust God without having a specific reason. Just know if you put God first, all your basic needs will be met; and if you can't make it happen after your needs are met, I don't know what to tell you.

What pisses you off?

Ignorance. I know there are a lot of things in life that we are ignorant about, because ignorance is just not knowing. But individuals that are ignorant and care nothing about reversing their ignorance irritate me. It really gets under my skin when someone purposely doesn't want to learn something, but they still complain about it. To me, you either do something about it, learn something about it, or shut up about it.

> "Nothing in this world is more dangerous than sincere ignorance and conscientious stupidity." —Dr. Martin Luthur King, Jr

What's one piece of advice you live by?

I have a few. In terms of achievement:

If you are persistent in life, you will get it. If you are consistent in life, you will keep it.

For rough patches in life:

Difficult times can define you, diminish you, or develop you. You decide.

Lastly, regarding patience and the creative process, I have a simple cliché:

Don't be in a rush to put out music that no one is waiting on.

What's one quality people reading this chapter should adopt from you?

My ability to get along with different people from all walks of life. It's simple: treat others how you want to be treated.

What's something you want the readers to take away from this chapter or your story?

Focus in life on what matters most—whether that be your passions or someone you love. No matter what that is, the end result will always be happiness.

You said One Man Band is a lifestyle. Could you explain how the readers could adopt it into their everyday lives?

I walk to the beat of my own drum, and anyone reading this should do the same. That's the way of the One Man Band. Being a leader and trendsetter is all about being comfortable in your own skin.

Why is promoting education so important to you?

I'm from Jackson, MS, where a large portion of Black men don't graduate high school, and even fewer graduate from college. While a lot of people I grew up with overcame those statistics, a lot more were impacted by inadequate education. A good education is the most important gift we can give to our youth. It's what helped me get to where I am today, and I just want more people (especially those back home) to receive a fair chance at all that life has to offer.

To be clear, when I talk about education I'm not just alluding to school; I'm referring to educating yourself on your craft as well. I'm promoting overall education; no matter what your path is, just get educated. For instance, I educate myself all the time on the history of drums. It's my craft, so I'm always trying to learn as much as I can about it.

> "Education is the passport to the future, for tomorrow belongs to those who prepare for it today." —Malcolm X

During our conversation you mentioned, "Everything is about relationships." Could you explain what you meant?

I guess I should've explained a little deeper. That statement is about good relationships and the fruits they can bear. I can only speak from my perspective, but I've received many blessings from the relationships I've cultivated with the various people who came into my life or crossed my path. As I said earlier, I treat people with the same respect that I'd want for myself. I've met and learned so much from people from so many different walks of life. That old saying is really true: the people you associate with now will determine your future. My relationships have given me constant inspiration, motivation, and a wealth of positive influence.

What's something you hear that is often misinterpreted?

The saying "Stay dangerous," is so misused and misinterpreted. It's not meant in terms of hurting someone. The premise is to keep your mind dangerous. Keep reading the next book, taking the next class, going to the next networking event etc. You want people to say, "That's a dangerous man (or woman)."

> "The secret of getting ahead is getting started. The secret of getting started is breaking your complex overwhelming tasks into small manageable tasks, and then starting on the first one." **—Mark Twain**

CHAPTER 7

ALWAYS NETWORKING

Ashlee On-Air

Instagram and Twitter: @ashleeonair

*"Whether you tell yourself you
can or you can't, you're right."*

Careers rise and fall daily based solely on people's ability to pull equity from past relationships or foster new ones, which makes networking truly essential to achieve success and influence. As I searched for the ideal person to showcase the power of networking, my old friend Ashlee Young came to mind. When it comes to networking and building influence, she is top tier. Currently, she's a program director and on-air personality for 93.7 The Beat, the leading hip-hop radio station in Houston, TX. I decided Ashlee would be the perfect person to talk to about networking because I have been following her journey since we met in Miami a few years back. Since then, I have been amazed by her ability to concentrate her forces to build her network and influence.

Ashlee wasn't always in this position. Over the years, she's had a plethora of jobs ranging from Starbucks barista to Blockbuster movie expert before ultimately settling into her role as a radio programmer and nationally syndicated radio host. All of this came through relentless work, effort, and networking.

Besides her obvious achievements, Ashlee has a compelling story that is sure to motivate and get you networking. She grew up in Tacoma, Washington, which is also home to Isaiah Thomas and Jamal Crawford. But as Ashlee is quick to let you know, "No one is from Tacoma." She was raised by her grandmother, a strict Southern Baptist from the Deep South—Gilmer, TX, to be exact. In an attempt to keep a young Ashlee from being influenced by the outside world, there was a strict no TV rule in her grandmother's house until she was 11 or 12 years old. Although she didn't know it at the time, going without television laid the foundation for her career in the entertainment industry. In those early years, she had to lean on the radio as her only outlet.

"As a kid, I can't really remember what my favorite station was, but I remember I would call in almost every day. I loved that station."

She spent countless nights listening to the night jocks and the morning personalities on Seattle's #1 station for hip-hop, KUBE 93.3, and this time played a vital role in shaping her. It taught her how to be entertaining and funny. She recalls not being able to watch BET or MTV until she was 13 years old, but when she started, she sat up all night to watch.

"I would be in a trance watching *106 & Park*, *TRL*, and documentaries like *Diary* or *Behind the Music*. While going through this period of deprivation from pop culture, she relied on her best friend and Limewire for her musical needs, including burned CDs.

"I had to get crafty listening to music, because my grandmother was strict," she explained. "But it all came together when 50 Cent dropped 'Wanksta.'"

That was the moment she fell in love with hip-hop after being suppressed most of her early life. Now she couldn't get enough. And so the journey began. She always felt naturally introverted, but in high school she decided to branch out and began doing the daily broadcast announcements.

"That decision put me on my path to be a journalist," she said.

That path led to her breaking barriers—Ashlee is the youngest programmer at iHeartRadio and one of only four Black women. She is syndicated in seven markets, and her show airs right after *The Breakfast Club*. However, what often goes unnoticed on her rise from small town Tacoma is her hustle and keen ability to build and maintain relationships.

I met Ashlee at the Revolt Music Conference (RMC) in Miami back in 2015. At the time, I was managing artists, so I went to the conference to network. But being shy, I ended up sitting at a table the whole time.

Ashlee walked over to the table and said something to the effect of, "Hi I'm Ashlee. I'm networking—what do you do?"

At that moment I could tell that she was serious about this. Here I was scared, and there she was brave and working the room. We talked, exchanged information, and talked about the industry. She explained that she volunteered at RMC in 2014 and before that she started as a digital intern at Clear Channel in Jacksonville, Florida.

She knew she wanted to get on-air, and she fully believed in herself, but to do so is no small feat. "At that level, nobody is gonna ask, 'Hey you wanna be on-air?'" But it was one of her early mentors, DJ Q45, that pushed her to start developing her craft.

There's this saying, "you get on by carrying crates." It comes from back in the days when music was consumed on physical records, and if someone wanted to learn how to DJ, they would ask the DJ if they could "carry crates." This was the person's chance to learn and soak up the game from someone they respected.

This is commonplace in the industry. For example, in his book *The Hollywood Commandments*, Devon Franklin explains this even clearer. He describes the importance of offering service and providing value as a gateway into the industry. He used to drive cars for Will Smith just to spend time around him to learn and grow.

Ashlee is a fan of the book and shared that, "It taught me that it's more about creating value and developing meaningful relationships over anything else."

Relationships are important, but something that's equally as important is putting in the work. "Putting in the work got me noticed," Ashlee said.

Here's what she means by that. In radio, you learn quickly that most people are in this for clout. "My first day as an intern, Rick Ross came through the station to promote his album *Mastermind*," she said. "He came with so much Belaire and WingStop, and that's all most people want—free food, drinks, wings, and a couple of pictures. It's that lifestyle that most people are interested in, but I have news for anyone interested in radio: the pay is shit when you are starting out."

Nevertheless, Ashlee networked and hustled her way into her current job. She met her boss at a networking event and told him, "Hey, I wanna learn how to use these software programs our company uses." He agreed to teach her, but she'd have to drive to Houston to learn the ins and outs of the program. Without hesitation, she agreed.

There was a period of time where Ashlee was in Houston so much, I thought she lived there. But it turns out that at least twice a month for a full year, she drove to Houston from College Station, TX—a 90 minute drive each way—just to learn how to use the programming software and the strategy that accompanies it. To give some perspective, the program she insisted on learning controls every radio station in the company. It was also her way of learning to program music from one of the greats. Because of that decision to commute back and forth to Houston, her boss was able to see her determination and offered her a position locally.

But why learn programming when you are an on-air personality? "Here's the thing," she said, "I love being an on-air personality, but it's fickle." In radio, they call being on-air "in front of camera." Although you aren't literally in front of a camera, in most cases, it's still a very visible role and, as she explains it, in those types of roles you only have as many good years as you are good to the people. Once you aren't part of the culture or a part of these big moments, you become irrelevant to the people and the culture.

In other words, once you are no longer hot, your job is in jeopardy and that is exactly what pushed her to learn how to program. "It's something I want to build a career on, whether in front of the camera or behind it," she explained. "I actually enjoy the work—it is the results and winning that I enjoy the most."

As I sat in this beautiful office space, I thought back to our conversation in Miami. I thought, "Who knew that maintaining this relationship for all these years would have landed me in the iHeart building in the heart of Houston, TX?"

That stop in Miami was one of the early pit stops of her career and mine. She said the journey has been hard. "It's been a lot of work," she recounted. "A lot of sacrifice—missing graduations, reunions, birthdays, and holidays all takes a toll on you. But for me, it is all worth it."

She is well on her way to achieving her dream of being a media mogul and scaling her brand to the likes of Ryan Seacrest and Nick Cannon. But according to Ashlee, her dreams still begin with hard work, obsession, and a lot of networking.

Please enjoy my conversation with Houston's very own, Ashlee On-Air.

What is the worst advice you hear given in your industry?

This is purely my opinion, although nothing so far has changed my mind. I hate the saying, "Don't ever burn bridges because you may have to cross them." I always say, I can burn bridges because I know how to swim. There are going to be people that backstab you or don't do good business, and because of who they are connected to or who they know, you are supposed to act a certain way. That's not me—I can swim.

I've had situations where people don't like me because I outshined them on a project we were working on together, and they went behind my back and showed my boss screenshots of my tweets hoping to get me fired. They said things like, "Look she's not being professional." This industry really shows you how your success triggers other people's insecurities and brings out the worst in them. I've had friends start rumors about me to end my career, and if you think I'm going to utilize that person again you trippin—they are getting blocked! As a matter of fact, if I see them, it's on sight.

Seriously, it's sad because a lot of times people get insecure when you start to outshine them, but they could just as easily say "Teach me." Ego is the biggest problem people have. So instead of asking for help, they just do some underhanded shit to get ahead, and now it's "fuck you" forever.

What's one quality you wish people could adapt from you?

I have two. One is going into things wanting to learn. Instead of asking what you can get from a person, ask what you can learn from them.

My second quality is corny, but it's really how I feel: my work ethic is unmatched. I never talk about it publicly, but deep down I feel like nobody can fuck with me on my work ethic. I will outwork you. It doesn't matter what it is.

I've never told anyone this story before. I remember two years ago, before I got hired, I was invited to this conference in Miami hosted annually by the urban division of iHeart. This was at a time when I wasn't really making any money. You know how expensive Miami is—you've stayed at the Fontainebleau, and this conference was at the Eden Roc hotel next door. Long story short, I couldn't afford it, but I was determined to figure out a way to make it work. I knew it would be the perfect networking opportunity, so I had to go.

I decided to rent a room—or more accurately, a bunk bed—at a hostel. A hostel is basically like a dormitory where you can rent a bed. But it's actually worse, because you don't know who the people are in the other bunk beds. I only had enough money to pay $30 a night for a room, but it was my golden opportunity to learn, network, and see how the industry worked. Those events are exclusive, and I was honored to be invited, so I had to figure out a way to show up.

So going back to your question—it's my work ethic. I will always outwork people. That's like the one thing I'm confident in. That, and if I don't know the answer, I will find it. If I have to read up on it, watch a YouTube video, find a mentor— it doesn't matter. I'm going to do whatever it takes. So I'd say, adopt those things and don't let anything stop you from your goals and dreams.

What is your best networking advice?

Honestly, networking is one of those things you have to just get out there and do. I'm a perpetual student, as most people should be. But people's egos won't let them accept this—it won't let them acknowledge that someone is more successful than them.

It really comes down to something simple: never stop evolving and always ask yourself, "Why not?" I excel in networking simply because I ask every person "What can you teach me?" or "What can I learn from you?" Just remember: the goals you create are dependent on the knowledge you have.

What is the best advice your parent(s) gave you?

As I mentioned earlier, I was raised by my grandma and she's as country as they come. She always told me, "Whatever doesn't kill you makes you stronger." It's a cliché, but it has always stuck with me. As a matter of fact, it was the quote I chose for my high school yearbook. It may not seem like it, but that really applies to life. I think back to all the things I've been through in my career; all of the stressful situations didn't break me, they made me stronger.

You know southern parents and grandparents are simple; they give you simple little anecdotes to get you through life. My drive comes from my grandmother. She always tells me to get back up. She's tough—I've seen her kill snakes with her bare hands. That's that Gilmer, TX, for you.

What keeps you in the music industry?

Representation. There aren't a lot of women in the music industry or radio. In a lot of ways, I'm lucky to work for the urban division of iHeart because our staff is predominantly Black; but there are still not a lot of women. Out of 850 stations, there are maybe five or six Black female programmers. Let me tell you why that's so crazy: our core radio audience is Black women, yet we are barely part of the conversation on the corporate level. Black women drive the decisions the executives make. If they like Summer Walker, the radio is gonna ensure we all like Summer Walker. I mean, if we're being honest, Black women have given Drake a 10-plus year career.

Not only are there very few Black women in this industry, but there aren't a lot of women in general. In a lot of ways, it's not just a Black or white thing—it's a gender issue. Even in the Top 40 division, whose target audience is 18-34 year old white women, it's still male-dominated—just white. It's run by white men over the age of 40, and that's why representation is important to me.

It's something I feel like I have been preparing for my whole life—I have always dreamt of this. Lala [Anthony] was the first woman that looked like me who was doing what I wanted to do. But once I got my foot in the door, I quickly learned that most of these labels are made up of mostly men. You rarely see women in the CEO position. There is no representation for women, let alone Black women. So, to an extent, this is something that drives me. I had an early mentor sit me down and explain that no one is going to give me anything. If I want it, I'm going to have to work for it.

> "Success isn't about how much money you make; it's about the difference you make in people's lives." **—Michelle Obama**

What are some of your favorite book recommendations and why?

How to Win Friends & Influence People by Dale Carnegie

I credit much of my networking success to this one book alone. This book taught me to be genuine and personable, and it also helped me with my on-air personality. If you stop looking to improve on-air, you'll get too mechanical and that can be disastrous. It also gave me confidence to walk up to people who are 20x my net worth and make a positive impression on them. Because of the line of work that I'm in, I interview a lot of influential people and artists. I didn't know how to move in those circles, but if I wanted to be successful I had to learn.

I'm not from a well-to-do family, so I didn't learn the language of the wealthy growing up. Before I got in the industry, I was never put in professional situations—I worked at Starbucks slangin' lattes. I had no formal training on how to be in a room with Diddy, let alone insert myself and add value to the conversation. People can tell when you aren't used to being in those rooms because you lack confidence. *How to Win Friends and Influence People* gave me a clean slate; it taught me to forget everyone's net worth and their title and talk to them like the person they are. You can ruminate on things so much that you psych yourself out. But honestly, it's not that deep.

Positioning by Al Ries and Jack Trout.

This book completely changed the game for me. I recommend this book to everybody, even strangers. There's a lot of psychology that goes into radio and programming. We play certain songs because we are trying to get into the mind of the listener. The whole goal of radio is to make you listen to us longer than the next station, so we are trying our best to keep you from changing the station. In order to do that, we have to understand people and their tastes. That's where this book shines, it's a marketing book, but it really teaches you how to position yourself and how to make decisions that will stick with people longer.

It also helped me build my brand. There's a french term called, "cherchez le créneau" which means "search for the hole." The next step is to fill it. When I first came to Houston, *Positioning* taught me to look for what was missing, so I found the hole and I filled it. For instance, the main thing that was missing in the radio landscape was interviews. There was no *The*

Breakfast Club of the south. I thought, "I'm a journalist, a hip-hop head, and I have a ton of connections." I reached out to my connections and told them to send anybody passing through Houston to the station so I could interview them. All the artists come to Houston because they want to get a grill from Johnny [Dang].

Additionally, I noticed the local team wasn't big on social media, so I filled that void. I'm young, so I started uploading my interviews to YouTube and Instagram. Then as I kept growing and more people started to notice, before I knew it I was interviewing Megan Thee Stallion, DaBaby, Yella Beezy, and others. That's the power of networking, finding a niche, and filling it.[2]

You've said before that Charlamagne tha God kept you in radio with one phone call. Can you explain?

At the time, I was working like crazy just for an opportunity. I was at the station all the time and going to the networking events and nothing was happening. When you try really hard, you have to see some type of progress to keep you going—we need that as people. But I was at that point you reach when it seems that things are just not working, so you start to question whether or not you should really be doing this. I had quit my salaried job at Target to follow my dream, and now I was starting to feel like that was a huge mistake. I mean, I was extremely close to calling them to ask for my job back. I asked God for a sign, because every time I was about to quit, something just kept telling me, "You should really be doing this."

---

2. Author Note: On Twitter, Ashlee also recommended *The ONE Thing* by Gary Keller, and I found it to be a perfect solution for anyone struggling with focus.

It's funny you asked this because Charlamagne texted me about this the other day basically saying, "I'm proud of you. I see how many stations you are on, and I remember when you wanted to quit."

Anyway, before I turned in my two week notice, I decided to email him. I had emailed him a few times in the past and he had never responded, but I decided to try one last time. I was out for ice cream with a girl from my competing station when I received a reply from him. I showed it to her and was like, "Yo WTF, he responded!"

He was like, "Yo what's up, call me tomorrow," and he gave me his number. I still have that email to this day.

When I called him—which happened to be on his birthday—he answered and said, "Yo whats up, I listened to your air check and it's a nice start. Everyone sucks in the beginning."

From there, I just got right to it and asked him for advice. This was before his book *Black Privilege* came out, so he explained to me what his journey was like and proceeded to shoot it to me straight. "Yo, if this is what you wanna do, you gotta make it happen," he said. "Stop questioning yourself, and go for it."

I shared with him that I literally had my two weeks notice typed up and was about to go back to Target. "Nah, just keep going," he encouraged, "Keep doing what you have to do."

Then he added, "You need to change your mindset. Read *Ask and It Is Given* by Esther Hicks and Jerry Hicks. I think you're looking at this from the clout-chasing standpoint. You want everyone to know your name, to see the accolades, and you want to get popular interviews."

After I thought about it, there may have been some truth to that. After that he basically told me to ask myself what I was willing to sacrifice to be the best. He ended, "You are either going to make the sacrifice, or you're not. If not, back out now and go do something else."

Since that convo, he has been one of my mentors. I made the sacrifice and bet on myself, and after I spent the next year of my career doing every job imaginable, I earned my position as an on-air programmer for KKYS and KVJM in College Station, TX. I joke with him all the time and say, "Thanks for keeping me out of that red and khaki, bro."

What are two pieces of advice you'd offer for anyone reading this chapter?

First, God puts weight on the shoulders of those who can carry it. That's also something my grandmother taught me. Everybody goes through things—whether personal or professional—but you have to be mentally strong and remind yourself that you can handle it. You were given this test because you needed to face it. Remember you can't go over it, you have to go through it.

Second, I love Scooter Braun and he always says, "Network with the people who are coming up with you." That's some real advice. It's not about reaching the richest or the number one person in your field, it's about building that trust with the people you came up with. If all you focus on is the big celebs, you are going to miss the people who really make things move.

Don't always look at the star or the point guard, look at the team. What you will find is that normally the most powerful people on the team are the body guard, the manager, the DJ, etc.

Scooter also says, "You get paid for the bullsh*t, everything else is free." Live by this!

Is there any wisdom you live by?

It's kind of funny, but it's so true. I always say, "When worst comes to worst, just sit down, drink your water (preferably alkaline), and mind your business."

There are going to be times when you will go through drama, but when you have real control over your emotions is when you can achieve real nirvana or "unfuckwithableness." I started to realize that people want to get that power over you or make you mad, but when you mind your business, people really start to see how petty they are.

I heard Karen Civil say, "I'm not going to step over a dollar for a penny." That stuck with me, and I'm also pretty big on manifestation. When you are aligned and living in your purpose, you won't feel like arguing on Twitter all day. To me, the highest level of serenity comes from controlling your emotions and not letting things get to you.

What's most important in achieving your dreams: passion or skill?

I always want people to follow their passion or whatever it is they care about, but passion isn't enough. I saw someone tweet, "Talent is not enough in this industry," a while back, and I couldn't agree more. The golden rule is marketing beats talent.

I'm a product of skill. Your book is for dreamers, but what's important is doing something about it. Someone can say, "I wanna be an astronaut," but the question is what are they doing to become one.

I believe in skills and marketing. I also believe that putting together a plan of action will get you further than, say, just being a good singer would. There are a million great singers, but for some reason Taylor Swift is one of the few selling a million records.

You tweeted, "If you're not obsessed with your 'passion' then you shouldn't be doing it." Do you still feel that way?

100%. Everyone's path is not going to be the same. However, I can say that everyone I know who is extremely successful is 100% obsessed with what they do. I keep one of my old Target name tags on my refrigerator at home to remind me of how much I hated it. I remember calling out sick because I hated going to work; that's when I knew it wasn't for me.

If you don't love what you put out into the world, you are going to end up hating it and wanting to quit. But radio taught me that if you really want to be great—or even a G.O.A.T.—you will put in the hard work every day. Obsession is necessary if you want to be great.

What is something you want to leave the reader with?

I would say, know this: If I—a girl from Tacoma, WA, who didn't come from a wealthy family—can make it and live out her dreams, so can you. This is the biggest cliché, but it's honest. You are what you think you are. If you think you aren't going to make it you won't.

I always tell myself that if people like 50 Cent and Nipsey Hussle can make it from their situation, after all the shit they went through, I can too. It's not a matter of luck, it's about believing in and betting on yourself. Whether you think you can or you can't, you're right.

> "I hate the word potential. Once you start getting older people don't care about your potential, they care about your results."
> **—Pastor Gary Brandenburg**
> of One Community Church in Plano, TX.

CHAPTER 8

FINANCIAL LITERACY

Greg Brumfield, Esq. of Financial Knife and Fork

Instagram: @financialknifeandfork
Twitter: @Financial_kf

*"Geniuses are made every day through
self-education and hard work."*

To paraphrase, Francis Bacon once said, "Money is a great slave, but a terrible master." In other words, if you are intentional with your money, it will serve you well. However, if you let your money control you, it will do so in miserable ways.

Dream wouldn't be complete without some financial advice, considering the fact that roughly 80% of Americans are caught in the chains of debt. It's time we ask ourselves how we can break this cycle and regain control of our finances, and more importantly, our lives. Ending your sleepwalk through life because of your financial troubles can be truly fulfilling. But before we embark on this journey of financial literacy, let me be clear—this chapter isn't to ridicule you about your financial ignorance, but instead to lift you and show you that you aren't alone.

With that said, meet Greg, the owner and operator of the social media account Financial Knife and Fork. His platform is focused on ending the paycheck to paycheck cycle for Black people and millennials. Greg was once in a position very familiar to many individuals trying to find their way in this world. Raised by a working class family in New Orleans, he understands the struggle of generational poverty. In our interview, he confided that he used to see his parents have explosive fights, which almost always stemmed from issues regarding money. As he describes it, "There was plenty of love in my home, but we struggled a lot; and like many families, there were times of financial tension and times of uncertainty where we stretched meals to get by."

Like many of us, finances weren't talked about in his household, but he didn't blame his parents for their shortcomings. He understood they did the best they could with the knowledge they had during the times they lived. Instead, he focused on the positive lessons they instilled, such as working hard. "They always told me if you work hard, you will make something good of yourself."

Greg, an employment attorney by trade, seems to have done just that. But after hitting a low and pulling himself up, he decided to take his newfound knowledge and educate "his people." Being truly passionate about financial literacy, he set his sights on spreading the word with one goal in mind: closing the racial wealth gap. Like many of you reading this, I had never heard of the wealth gap and had no idea how it directly affected us. So, as any good journalist would, I did my research. Here's what I found.

The most important fact about the racial wealth gap is that it starts with us. Sure, this situation was forced on us in many ways, but just like the U.S, life doesn't give reparations. What we must do now is educate ourselves on the wealth gap and its history, and then pass those lessons along to future generations.

During my first chat with Greg, he insisted that I watch "Explained: The Racial Wealth Gap," which is a Vox documentary that can be found on Netflix and YouTube. As I sat and watched this documentary multiple times, I was stunned by how far behind we truly were. This led me down a rabbit hole of research that uncovered some pretty harsh truths.

Let's say the wealth gap started at the end of slavery, which is being modest at best. At the end of this dark day, something critical happened that is often overlooked or purposely hidden: additional land, tax credits, and debt forgiveness was extended to many Americans. In many cases, in order to receive these benefits, you had to be a homeowner. Because of this caveat, many negroes were excluded because very few—if any—owned a home in a post-slavery society. So with no home or land, Black people were forced out of one terrible situation into another. This is one of the key moments we can point to when looking for the origin of the wealth gap.

The promise of "40 acres and a mule" by the government was quickly reversed because it was said to be unfair to white Americans. So the negro received nothing but a mountain of trauma and unfulfilled promises.

Think of it this way. Let's say your family was privileged enough to buy a modest plantation in Greg's hometown of New Orleans, Louisiana in 1869. By "modest," I mean a plantation equipped with a home, servant rooms, several out houses, and a garden. All of this sitting on roughly 15 acres of land, 2 of which sit on the Mississippi river with an additional 13 acres primed for agricultural development. The price: $15,000 cash; or a yearly payment of $1000. That investment of $15,000, would be worth at least $227,184.05 today. Imagine having that kind of wealth in your family from birth—the opportunities would be endless. Your family could use the equity to take out a loan against the home to start a business, pay for college, or pay down debt from harvesting the land for profit. Scenarios like this are exactly how the wealth gap began to rapidly widen.

As Greg put it, "Two things lead to wealth in this country: homeownership and stock ownership." Believe me when I say, it doesn't take more than 15 minutes of research to realize that homeownership used to be—and in many ways still is—damn near impossible for many Black Americans. With banks betting on you to fail by issuing loans with unfavorable terms, coined "ghetto loans," it's not hard to see how we have been financially suppressed for so long. Although we have more opportunity now, we are still very much behind, making it that much more important for us to continue to push the culture forward.

Greg started his journey for that exact reason—he wanted to spread knowledge because these things aren't taught in school. He decided that if we were ever to catch up, someone needed to learn the rules of wealth creation and explain them clearly. As Greg says, it isn't about getting lucky, "It's about making prudent decisions consistently over time. Mix good decisions and compound interest, and you are almost certain to become a millionaire at some point."

To be direct, Greg isn't referring to being rich. To him wealth is what you own minus what you owe, commonly referred to as your net worth. Unfortunately, a lot of us are born into generational poverty from the poor choices of those before us. As frustrating as that may be, you can't fault the people before you for making bad choices when they had very limited information. Continuing to hold on to the bad hand you were dealt doesn't have to be your story. Every day you have the chance to get up and change the course of your life. It's hard work, but doable.

My hope is that this book, and specifically this chapter, allows you to dust yourself off, assess the situation, and formulate a plan that works for you. Everyone's journey is going to be different because there are so many variables that contribute to the situation. You have to be honest and ask yourself what you want the next 10, 20, and even 30 years of your life to look like. I know changing old habits is tough work, but it's doable. Trust me; you got this.

I hope you enjoy this conversation with Greg.

Have you experienced being in debt? If so, what led you there?

Like most people, it really all started in college. I got my first credit card in the mail one day and it had a $1500 dollar limit. That was more money than I had ever had. Then one day in law school, I got a letter saying, "We increased your credit line to $5500." I remember that moment like it was yesterday, because I maxed that card out quickly. I say that's where it started because things went left quickly. You would think things would have gotten better once I started my new job, but that wasn't the case.

I was fresh out of law school and blessed with an opportunity to work at a really high-profile law firm. They started me off with a generous salary (I was making around 100K). You have to realize, I'm a hood kid. I'm not from a good neighborhood, I went from having nothing to getting paid more money every two weeks than I had ever seen at any point in my life. So being a young kid from New Orleans, that "Cash Money Lifestyle" got the best of me. I felt like I had to make up for lost time, so I bought all the Jordans and clothes I could never afford. I was in Saks every week, and to keep financing my lifestyle, I started applying for more credit cards. Before I knew it, my credit card debt had risen to over $25,000.

It became crippling, because it all started to hit at once. I had credit card debt, student loans, and I was living in a place where I was paying for more rent than I needed. On top of all of this, I wanted to get married, so the only way I could do that was to finance my wife's ring. Just like that, my spending habits set in and I began living above my means. Before I knew it, the tab on all of this stuff came due, and I was stuck with all of this credit card debt and my student loan payments began rolling in. I went from having the most money I ever had, right back into that cycle that keeps us down. It was my financial illiteracy that landed me here.

What are some of the steps you took to start overcoming debt?

I sought financial literacy. I woke up one day and I was pissed at myself and my situation. I was so fed up that I decided to park myself at Barnes and Noble for about four weekends in a row. I read every financial magazine and book, and as I learned things, I would immediately start applying my new found knowledge to my financial situation.

One of the first things I did was call one of my creditors

and have them suspend my credit card. That keeps you from using it, and in some instances you stop interest from accruing. I would then take that payment and apply it to one of my credit cards with a lower payment so that I could pay that one off quicker. Once I eliminated one credit card, I would rotate the funds to another one, and I kept doing that until I paid them off.

You can also do something similar with your car loan. Call the institution and have them grant you an extension. Basically what you are doing is using your money from other places to pay down other debt to help you free up more money to attack some of your bigger debts. (This method is sometimes referred to as the snowball method). The main thing is that once you pay off a debt, you need to use that freed up money to pay down another debt. For instance, I was paying $330 a month for my car note. When I paid off my car, instead of pocketing that extra money, I used it to pay off other debts.

You have to be intentional with your money and you have to want to get out of debt. Unless you are in survival mode—living paycheck to paycheck—you should use that free money to attack other debts. If you are in survival mode, I recommend you start working on your emergency savings first. That way, if you fall on hard times, at least you will have some sort of cushion.

You mentioned emergency savings—what's the importance of that?

It's a must! I go through 12 steps on my Financial Knife and Fork platform. I usually say start with your retirement, something like a 401K, because it's a built-in emergency savings. But your emergency savings is the money you put up for a rainy day. The rule of thumb is to save enough to cover six months of whatever your expenses are. But honestly in these conditions you don't know what could happen. Your job could move or you could be furloughed, so I say you need to start with six months, but you should shoot to be closer to a year. That way if something happens, you are not forced to take a job you don't want. You can regroup and buy yourself some time.

What is the first thing you recommend to people?

Pay off your debt. When you are trying to get ahead, you need to have your money working for you, and that's hard to do when you are in debt. You can't get ahead when you are paying out more than you are bringing in. Debt and inflation are the main things that attack your earnings. Once you get debt out of the way, you can really begin to see your money grow. To be clear, I'm not saying I don't have any debt; you have to make a distinction. I have a mortgage and I'm still paying off my student loans. Outside of the student loans, a mortgage would be considered "good debt." Things like a car loan can also be considered good debt.

For instance, if you just have a car note and no credit card debt, I think that's fine. At that point, you can begin to start putting money into your retirement or investing. But let's say you have credit card debt or high interest loans. You want to get stuff like that knocked out first because you are paying more in interest than the actual purchases you made. So I always recommend getting your "bad debt" out of the way first, then start working on your retirement. And once you have a good retirement plan in place, I would recommend looking into investing or some other stream of income.

You've mentioned retirement, specifically a 401K, a few times. Can you explain what that is?

In its simplest form, a 401K is a retirement vehicle. I wouldn't get so caught up in the title; some people have a 401B, but it's the same mechanism. Basically, you put money into it pre-tax, and in some cases employers match. It builds up over time, and you are compounding interest on this until you retire. The reason I talk about retirement so much is because it's more important now than ever. If you don't put money into some sort of retirement vehicle and you don't have a pension, then you are really just counting on Social Security and your savings. And that's going to put you in a tough situation. Personally, I don't trust Social Security for our generation. It's looking very sketchy and is due to run out in the 2030s. That means the importance of establishing good financial practices and building a solid foundation is more important now than it's ever been. If there's no Social Security and you don't have a 401K or some serious savings, you're going to be 80 years old working at Walmart to survive.

What is some of the worst financial advice you've heard?

That your retirement doesn't matter. I've heard people say they want to skip the process and go straight into investing, but that's not how you do these things. You have to be a disciplined investor, and in order to do that you have to not be emotionally tied to the cash you have invested. Simply put, you shouldn't have your life savings tied up in the market because it's too volatile. If you have your savings tied up in things like Forex, Bitcoin, or individual stocks that you are not confident in, you are going to pull your money out at inopportune times, thus losing you more money than you anticipated.

Let's say you have 10-20K in the market and a big dip occurs, similar to the one COVID-19 caused. If that investment drops to 3-4K, human nature is going to make you pull the money that's invested out. Now you're mad and jaded towards the market, and you won't get back in. Not getting back in will only limit your earning potential over the long run. When these dips occur—and trust me, they will—you need to be able to ride the ups and downs. That's exactly what being a disciplined investor is.

I read an article you tweeted. Summed up, it said, "Black families in the US have 90% less wealth than white families, and the gap has gotten larger over time." What should Black families be focusing on and do we have the tools?

Absolutely! The tool is financial literacy. That's what I'm always trying to tell people: you need to sit down and evaluate your finances. Once you have things in order, then you can start to take risks. Calculated and educated risks are what grow your money, but you would be working against yourself to try to take these risks before you have your affairs in order. Once you've done that, you can sit back and watch your money grow, which will inevitably bring more peace into your life and home. You should be intentional with your money, but you also need to be honest with yourself about the choices that keep you in whatever cycle you can't break free from.

Historically, what do you think has hurt Black families the most in terms of finance?

Not wanting to talk about it—especially men. We don't want to be looked at as a "broke boy" or someone who can't provide. In our culture, that's seen as a sign of weakness. I remember when I was struggling, I wouldn't tell my friends, and I damn sure wouldn't tell someone I was dating.

You said something earlier, "Let me know if I'm being too invasive." When I heard that, I thought, "That's exactly what we need." We need to be even more invasive. Finances are so hush-hush, especially in the Black community. If we don't start talking about these things, we will never be able to overcome them.

Can financial literacy really make or break entrepreneurs?

I believe it can. For someone who wants to be an entrepreneur, managing money properly is a huge step and a skill that they must learn. You need to have that literacy in your mind because for every winner you see out there on Instagram, there are a whole lot more losers. If you can't manage money properly, that'll be just one more thing working against you. Now you'll be paying a failed business loan as you try to make it through life. It'll also hurt your credit, resulting in you not being able to get any loans in the future and continuing the cycle because you prematurely hopped into a bad business venture or didn't manage the business finances correctly. It's important to never take more than you need, and it's always wise to spend the funds carefully when starting your business.

What are your thoughts on investing over the next 10 years?

Over the next 10 years, anybody—especially those in their mid 20s or mid 30s—should invest in themselves both financially and in terms of knowledge. No matter your age, think about the future and your retirement.

Second, in terms of the stock market, I believe most people should start with ETFs and Index funds so that they can ease themselves into learning. Far too many new investors invest in individual companies before they have any basic conceptual knowledge. You should look at investing as if you were purchasing a piece of the company, which you are. In other words, if you are an avid Apple supporter, why put your hard earned cash into HP? My advice is to always stick with companies that you believe in and understand. But the market is a great place once you have your affairs in order because you want your assets to pay for your fun.

You talked about individual stocks versus ETFs and Index funds. Which do you recommend?

I wish I had started with Index funds or ETFs so I could have learned and eased myself in. But I learned through buying individual stocks. The downside to individual stocks is you don't get to spread your risk. With ETFs and index funds you get that safety net since they are made up of several different companies. You can see what's performing well and what isn't, but it won't affect your money entirely because the risk is spread out. Whereas, if you own an individual stock of say, Disney, when they are having a bad day or get hit with a bad headline, your account is going to feel any fluctuation in the stock price. ETFs and index funds give you a better chance to pick a company that's performing well and that you believe in.

When you decide to start buying individual stocks you should start looking at those companies closer. Ask questions like, "How are they growing my money?" But the key is listening to yourself and understanding that when purchasing individual stocks, you are purchasing a piece of the company and you need to be prepared to hold it for the long haul, through the ups and downs.

> "Never test the depth of the river with both feet." **—Warren Buffet**

In terms of finance, do you believe people shape their own reality?

I believe your steps are ordered, but you have to do the work. You can't let your background dictate your privilege. You don't have to be a genius—geniuses are made every day through self-education and hard work.

What are some of your favorite book recommendations and why?

First I want to say, finance isn't something that one book can fix. Instead it takes continual effort and a willingness to want better. But these are my favorite suggestions.

How to Retire with Enough Money by Theresa Ghilarducci

This book breaks down financial literacy in 100 pages in such plain talk. That's exactly what I want to do with Financial Fork and Knife. I took a lot of the principles in this book and pushed it to my people. Lawyers and finance people have a certain language they use that can be quite confusing, so it's refreshing to get some simplicity.

Outliers by Malcolm Gladwell

Through this book, I realized that a lot of these "special" people actually aren't that special. We all have it inside of us to succeed if we take the time to learn and follow certain steps.

What is more important in order to achieve your dreams: passion or skill?

For me, it's skill. If you can get to enough money, then you can do whatever you want to do and can truly follow your "passion." When you have a skill and you work to develop it, you will build something valuable that will make you money. Skills turn into money, money turns into freedom, and that freedom allows you to chase whatever it is that you are passionate about.

What would you like the reader to take away from our conversation?

That anybody can achieve financial freedom. It's nothing special—it's taking money to live on and saving some for yourself. If you do that, in as little as two years from now your life can be totally different. It's no secret that I consider myself a dreamer. I just needed to wake up and get my finances together.

AUTHOR NOTE:

"If you don't do anything else, start building your emergency savings, especially in this environment." That is one of the many great points that Greg made, and I want to end this chapter on a personal note. I know saving is hard and even harder to commit to, but saving is simply paying yourself first. Think about it; if you taxed yourself say 10% for all the bullshit you put yourself through during each pay period, it would be well worth it and you would cherish that 10% more.

Here's a suggestion vetted by yours truly. About 4 years ago, I read a book that changed my life with money, *The Richest Man in Babylon* by George S. Clason. After reading the parables in the book, I decided to give this old man's wisdom a go and I started saving roughly 4% of my earnings. Before anyone and I do mean anyone: God, Uncle Sam, my wife, the local bar etc., I got my cut first!

After a few months, I was so impressed at how my saving power grew, I quickly upped it to 6%; then 10% and before I knew it I had gotten tighter with my money and it started to compound. Just like that, I was able to pay off more debt, do more nice things for my wife, and above all else—it made me feel good. More importantly, it made me feel self-sufficient, knowing that things life would inevitably throw at me could be overcome through discipline.

If you don't save, I don't judge. However, I strongly suggest you start. No matter when you read this book, you will be a day older tomorrow and that's a fact that should move you to start preparing for the future. It's better to start being intentional with your money now. In today's world, talking about retirement isn't sexy. With so many entrepreneurs vying to make a million dollars before 35, we overlook one important fact: each day we are getting older and closer to death. And if you are like me, I'd prefer to enjoy my last years comfortably and not worry about who I owe.

Hopefully, you will listen to Greg's advice and take control of your finances if you are indeed one of the many people struggling. Understandably, having an honest conversation about your finances is awkward. But trust me—the only way around the issue is by going through it.

> It doesn't interest me what you do for a living. I want to know what you ache for – and if you dare to dream of meeting your heart's longing. **–Oriah Mountain Dreamer**

CONCLUSION

Dreams can drive, haunt, or uplift us. Though they are many different things to people, for most they are "A cherished aspiration, ambition, or ideal." That definition was provided by Google, but it provides so much truth. This is usually what most mean when they say they have a dream. It's that ideal that has stuck with you through adolescence, or that aspiration you instantly fell in love with. Whatever it is, you care so much because it's yours. You've grown to cherish it, but the truth is, in order to turn that dream into something tangible, it takes a lot of hard work and ambition.

Dreams can be tricky and you must be on guard to ensure a smooth ride during your process. Let this alternative definition of "dream" settle in your mind before you move forward: "A state of mind in which someone is or seems to be unaware of their immediate surroundings." If you think about your immediate surroundings as your reality, you will see how this can be negative. If you cut off contact with reality while you are making strides towards your goals, you will likely burn out. Cutting off contact or being stubborn to the truths of your reality will only hurt you. We need to be open to correct our blindspots and save ourselves a lot of heartache, cash, and time. This is why it is so important to find a support system to lean on, be it a mentor or a good book. Your goal should be to seek knowledge at every step to keep yourself sharp.

Some people are reluctant to call themselves dreamers. Rightfully so; in a lot of ways, we are seen as people who don't get things done. The fact of the matter is, dreams are abstract; and maybe that's why most see dreamers as people who are living in a fantasy world, incapable of making any real progress towards their goals.

This is all false. Don't let anyone tell you what you can't do. This book laid out eight stories of people from eight different walks of life who overcame certain circumstances to create a career or lifestyle they approve of.

Whether you consider yourself a dreamer or not is your choice. My only hope is that this book has given you some words of encouragement, good advice, or some entertainment. The road to achievement doesn't have a concrete answer, so why should we believe our path to happiness, achievement, freedom, or fame will? I can bet with almost complete certainty that your path will be different from the path of the next person. But the advice in this book can help to lead you in the right direction.

Advancing with a sense of purpose, embracing failure, and taking care of your money are all cornerstones of a life well lived. But no matter where life takes you, always remember that you are all that you need to succeed. Be of integrity and confidence, and if people don't believe in you or won't lend a helping hand, create your own lane.

This book was designed specifically for anyone looking to

improve their circumstances and I hope this has been as helpful as I intended it to be. The insight from the innovators, trendsetters, and businesspeople was meant to provide guidance through whatever obstacles you may be facing. After pushing through less than favorable situations, these dreamers showcased adoptable qualities and wise reasoning. As I said in the beginning, all you need to make these ideas your own is a little creativity and patience.

I would love for this book to be something you pick up when you need some words of encouragement to keep pushing forward. I hope you find practical suggestions and thoughts that can bring a little more peace and happiness to your own life. I hope you realize that a dream doesn't always have to be tangible. Sometimes, our dreams are just that—a state of mind. Some people dream of a life of no worries, some of financial freedom, and some to be a jet-setting celebrity. The fact still remains that achieving those things comes from learning and mastering yourself. But that's the beauty of it. Dreaming should be euphoric, exciting, and exhilarating. The challenges and trials that come with chasing a dream make it fun.

So with all of this said, here's what I want you to do. I implore you to take two simple steps. First, start. This is typically the hardest part of pursuing a dream because we get lost in the details. We convince ourselves day in and day out that the task at hand is too big and too challenging, and we make excuses for why we will start tomorrow. No one ever starts tomorrow. You must be the person who starts today. If you've already started, then remain consistent. The old adage still stands, "If you are a painter, then you must paint."

Secondly, "clearly define the person you want to be."

Another life changing quote from *The Art of Living*. The author goes on to urge us to stop being vague and "explicitly identify the kind of person you aspire to become."

The truth is that I always aspired to be a millionaire by 30, and I realized early on that was the stem of a lot of my problems. As people, most of our problems are self-inflicted by barriers that we put around ourselves or boxes we put ourselves in. I don't want to get things confused—I am not saying becoming a millionaire shouldn't be your dream. All I'm saying is that for a period of my life, that was my dream. But once I started to focus on what made me happy and not the money, things started lining up in a divine way. Although I didn't become a millionaire by 30, becoming a self-published author filled the void. But I can say this: I genuinely believe if I had known and used half of the advice in this book in my early 20s, chances are I probably would be a millionaire by now.

My hope is that this book helps you explore yourself and audit your dreams with a little more perspective and clarity. In order to increase your clarity you have to return to some of the topics discussed to familiarize yourself with them and their usefulness and timelessness.

I really struggled with how to close this book. Honestly, I struggled with the idea of putting out a book of interviews. I questioned myself, "Why would people care?" Entrepreneurship and dreaming is depicted as free and thrilling, but the negative emotions from it are the ones that usually consume us. Chasing a dream can bring out your innermost panic, anxiety, depression, insecurity, and sometimes, rage. But you have to overcome these feelings to seek out your life's task. You have to realize that a lot of those opinions stem from our need to please others and to be accepted. Ask yourself these simple questions,

"Are you doing it for them or are you doing it for you?" Your answer should be you!

To end this book, I want to provide one of my favorite quotes from Marcus Aurelius. He provided this advice many years ago but it still remains true today.

> "It never ceases to amaze me: we all love ourselves more than other people, but care more about their opinion than our own."

Go out, decide what you want from life, and get it. Nothing is stopping you or holding you back. I don't know where my pen will take me, but I'm excited to find out. Don't just Dream, Dream Big!

ACKNOWLEDGMENTS

KRYSTLE EASLEY TAYLOR

"There's power in simplicity."

Thank you. Thank you for believing in me. Thank you for unconditionally loving me. Thank you for reading every piece I have ever written. Thank you for being a supportive wife. Thank you for being my friend. Most importantly, thank you for always being honest with me and allowing me to be myself. From the bottom of my heart, I love you.

TRAVERS JOHNSON

"Good books can be great mentors."

I will be brief: you are always quick to remind me that good books "get to the point." Thank you for the push every step of the way. I'm so glad we met in Miami. Here's to many more years of friendship and to the countless unwritten books that I hope to have you edit.

TO MY MOTHER, SANDRA "BAE BAE" TAYLOR

Sandra Faye, I love you! For those years I almost gave you a heart attack, I apologize; I was finding myself. I'm forever grateful for your love and support.. Thank you for everything you've done for me.

TO MY GRANDFATHER, REV JEFFREE TAYLOR, SR.

You are one of the best role models a young man could ever have. I see you and I see a man of impeccable character. I'm thankful for all of the wisdom you passed down. Until we meet again.

TO MY FAMILY

I truly believe I am a sum of all of the personalities I've been lucky to grow up around. From my aunts and uncles, to my cousins and nephews, and last but not least, my crazy siblings; I love you all more than words could ever express. I am grateful for every contribution you've made to me and to this book.

TO MY FRIENDS

Very fun times ahead. Thanks for listening to me vent about my frustration every step of the way and for encouraging me to keep writing. The love I have is unmatched. It might be cliché but as the saying goes, "Show me a man's friends, and I will show you the man." I'm confident.

www.ingramcontent.com/pod-product-compliance
Lightning Source LLC
Chambersburg PA
CBHW020910080526
44589CB00011B/518